SELLING SKILLS FOR COMPLETE AMATEURS

Bob Etherington

Marshall Cavendish
Business

Copyright © 2008 Bob Etherington

First published in 2008 by:

Marshall Cavendish Limited
5th Floor
32–38 Saffron Hill
London EC1N 8FH
United Kingdom
T: +44 (0)20 7421 8120
F: +44 (0)20 7421 8121
sales@marshallcavendish.co.uk
www.marshallcavendish.co.uk

The right of Bob Etherington to be identified as the author of this work has been asserted by him in accordance with the Copyright, Designs and Patents Act 1988.

A CIP record for this book is available from the British Library

ISBN 978-1-905736-45-4

Designed and typeset by Phoenix Photosetting,
Lordswood, Chatham, Kent

Printed and bound in Great Britain by
CPI Bookmarque, Croydon CR0 4TD

Contents

Introduction

"It's the hardest thing to do in the entire acting realm. You've got 24 seconds to introduce yourself, introduce the product, say something nice about it and get off gracefully." The words of an American named Dick Wilson. He was an actor not a salesman. But due to the uncertainty of permanent employment in his chosen profession, he started selling and became well known across the USA for his TV salesmanship promoting "Charmin", one of the most successful brands of toilet paper.

Dick was ninety-one when he died in November 2007 and, well into his old age, was still the face of Charmin and extremely wealthy. Not the most glamorous product in the world but a multimillion dollar market. Not how Dick dreamed of applying his talent but one of the most necessary activities in the world.

The book you have in your hands shows non-sales people (like you), exactly how to sell brilliantly (just like Dick) whenever the need arises.

I know you probably don't want to spend everyday of your working life *selling* anything. That's quite OK ... it's nothing unusual. That's why you do the job you do in your company and leave the selling to your trained sales people.

But the basic fact of business is that nothing happens in any commercial organization until somebody sells something. And until it's sold, your business doesn't need what you do every day. It doesn't need accountants, engineers, geologists, doctors, technicians, PAs, traders, dealers, actors, marketers, artists, designers, COOs, CEOs, MDs, CIOs, CTOs or Chairmen. Or, indeed, anybody else. Because the only thing that says you have a viable business is your answer to this question:

Do you have any customers?

You can sell a product or service long before you are actually in a position to deliver it. (I know because I have … many times and very successfully.) The much worse (and very common) position is to spend a fortune on offices, headed paper, computers, "product" and all the other office paraphernalia, then find you can't sell it. The hard truth is that for most markets in the world there is plenty of "product" out there. There is actually no global shortage of "product".

The area of international shortage is in people who know how to sell. And within that dearth an even bigger shortage of senior management, middle management, technical and support staff and other executives who have bothered to find out what persuades and what dissuades. When these non-sales executives (Amateur Sellers) get in front of customers they make professional sellers cry.

It is why you, as a "senior", will find this book a godsend. You will know "how" and your other management colleagues won't. You will be popular with your sales force, they will not. You will be welcome to attend customer meetings, they will not.

What this book gives you:

Insight.

Persuasive power.

Sales knowledge.

Even though knowledge is power, most managers and senior executives just don't have it when it comes to "selling". As a result they talk themselves and their company out of some excellent sales everyday because they don't know. Indeed "sales technique" is seen as something slightly underhand; even manipulative. An engineer in an entrepreneurial company which had just developed a new type of electronic X-ray "chip", told me so just a few weeks ago. I watched him addressing a room full of customers shortly afterwards.

His "sales spiel" was about co-valent bonding, "rads", electro-magnetic sensitivities, micro-volts and milliamps. Half an hour later, the emerging audience from all over Europe were visibly confused and shaking their heads. "I don't get it," said one man. "I just want to know, what's it all about? What will it do for me?"

The engineer had set out to "impress" with his technical knowl-edge. He had piled-up all his "technical" stuff in his PowerPoint sales presentation. At the end we, in the audience, had an idea that the product was a sophisticated X-ray chip. But what would it do? What problem did it set out to solve for us?

The answer was incredibly simple and wonderfully useful. Its brilliance was that it would allow X-ray images to be record-ed with 1/500 of the radiation power normally required for any X-ray. The uses for both industry and medical use were (and are) huge. But it took me ages to get him to explain this to me. In industry the manufacturers of mobile phones could examine 1000 phones an hour for circuit faults compared with the 100 currently possible on each factory line. In the medical world, hospital radiologists could see many more patients each day without the danger of radiation poisoning.

Yet none of this was mentioned during the previous presentation. The engineer left it to the audience to "see" the advantages. And they all failed to see what was under their noses. Millions of dollars disappeared out of that company's door that day.

And this happens every day in various businesses around the world.

Customers are not stupid but their brains are generally lazy.

It is the job of the professional seller (and the re-trained Amateur) to wake up the brains of potential customers as soon as possible. Before somebody (like me) comes in under your radar and steals your business from you.

Kick-start poster

To lead you straight into this I have provided you with a mini poster on the next page. It is a page which you can tear out of this book if you wish (once you've purchased it) and pin to the wall in front of you. Everything you need to know about "business persuasion" and selling is encompassed in the few words on that poster.

Understand this concept and you are home and dry. Not only that but your sales staff will think you're some sort of "Sales God".

What could be better than that?

I look forward to hearing about your success.

Bob Etherington

1. Tear here.
2. Pin to the wall in front of you.
3. Read the book.

Telling isn't Selling

Your customers place more value in the words that come out of their own mouths compared with anything they hear from yours.

Your customers place more value in the things they ask for, rather than the things you freely offer them which they didn't ask for.

Who sold you this then?

What's the answer, Ben? … How did you do it?

WILLY LOWMAN: (TRAGIC CENTRAL FIGURE IN ARTHUR MILLER'S
DEATH OF A SALESMAN) TO HIS SUCCESSFUL BROTHER BEN

In 1974 the comedian John Cleese made an excellent corporate training video. Its title was "Who Sold You This Then?" It was one of a number of training films released through his company Video Arts Ltd. The training objective of this particular film was to make service engineers and similar support staff, aware of how easy it can be to "unsell" a product or service once it has been sold and installed.

In one memorable scene Cleese (the service engineer) is attending a customer with a broken machine. He examines it for a few minutes and then gives his verdict: "You know what's wrong with this! You've been using it haven't you?!"

It makes us laugh mainly because we've all heard the same and similar remarks in real life. Peter Sellers, the comedy actor who used to play the incompetent French Detective Inspector Clouseau in the *Pink Panther* films, said that what made Clouseau funny was that he did stupid things seriously.

The real life problem (and the point of this book) is that real sales are often messed up by well meaning non-sales – and often very senior – executives saying things (seriously) to customers which are best left unsaid and doing things (seriously) which are better left undone. And all this before the sale has actually been closed!

OK let's cut to the chase ... Does anyone here actually know how to sell anything?

Yes ... the thing is ... the awful truth is ... dare I say it? ... OK here goes: these people (YOU?) are obviously very good at their day-to-day job but they simply don't know how to sell! And it's no joke.

Don't mention "selling" round here

I'm a long-term international salesman with a sales history stretching back into the 1970s. Nowadays I run an international sales training company mainly for the guidance of professional sellers. But I am often asked to provide "a few *pointers*" on effective, persuasive, selling skills to very successful non-sales people (CEOs, MDs, COOs, CIOs, CFOs, CTOs, plus software designers, engineers, geologists doctors, dentists, accountants, etc) who are about to meet prospective customers, clients or patients in their business. Sometimes they don't even mention the word "selling"; in many cases any hint of "selling" is a "big no-no". They prefer to call it, "informed consent" or "business persuasion" or "business development". (Oh dear … oh dear … oh dear!)

Sometimes these executives will be accompanying their professional sales staff on a meeting with a customer and sometimes they'll be doing it on their own but they all want to do it right. They are the wise ones. The few. The ones who recognize and seek assistance.

The majority, however, *think* they know … OH NO!

They spurn the pre-customer-meeting briefing. ("I want to meet a couple of clients next week when I'm in London/New York/Hong Kong/CapeTown, Bob … fix it up there's a good chap!") They arrange to meet in the customer's foyer. ("Good morning Bob … let's get this underway then! … just give me a bit of background as we go up in the lift.") They fail to realize the minefield they are about to enter.

Here are ten unintentional sales killers I've heard uttered at customers by "seniors" in the subsequent customer meetings:

   1. So how much more of a financial incentive can we offer you to make a decision *today*?

2. We are making you a very generous offer in this case.

3. Well of course you mention Acme Products who are a competitor of ours and their product is actually very poor quality.

4. You must understand the problem we have with our staff at the moment.

5. If I can be perfectly honest here …

6. Actually, we are *not* too expensive.

7. First I think you should know some history of our company [10 minutes "blah"] … and that's how we got where we are today.

8. We'll come back to your point later if we may. But first I want Bob to show you a PowerPoint presentation of all the things our company does.

9. Well that's a very interesting proposal. However let me tell you what **we** were thinking on our way to see you this morning.

10. Yes. If I can just stop you there. I think I know what you're going to say so let me tell you how we can address this type of issue you are experiencing.

These are just ten things. They're not even the top ten … they are just ten in common use that instantly come to mind.

If you are inclined to say them or blurt them (or anything like them) to your company's customers, you increase your chance of wrecking your sale by about 80%.

Here's an analysis of the damage these Amateur throwaway lines can cause:

Sales killer "Home Truths"

So how much more of a financial incentive can we offer you to make a decision *today*? The price of your product is rarely the main reason your customer has for buying or not buying your product. And 80% of price problems during a sale are caused by the seller "telling" too much. To quote the old maxim: "Telling isn't selling".

We are making you a very generous offer in this case. This is known in the trade as an "irritator". It is the type of highly dangerous phrase tossed around by well meaning non-sales people. The "good-intention" is to make the customer feel as if they are being treated as "special." (We are a customer centric organization.) But (oh dear!) in reality it actually has *precisely* the opposite effect; it makes your customer feel that you (the seller) are implying that they are not being equally "generous", "fair" or "reasonable".

Well of course you mention Acme Products who are a competitor of ours and their product is actually very poor quality. Never "knock" the opposition. If the customer is already a user of the product or service you are challenging their judgment in purchasing it in the first place. And if you are on record as having said anything negative it invariably gets back to the other company. You are not immune from this whoever you are. As US President Abraham Lincoln said, "It's not that I can't keep a secret. It's the people I tell them to who can't keep them."

You must understand the problem we have with our staff at the moment. Why? … Why should they understand? Whatever they say to you, your customers are actually only interested in themselves and *their* problems. Your problems are of little or no interest to them. You "the seller" have only one area of value: your ability to solve a problem. If you can't articulate that for any reason, your value slips towards zero.

If I can be perfectly honest here … This popular phrase instantly implies to your customer, at a deeply subconscious level, that you haven't been honest so far in the conversation. You might as well come straight out and say that you have had your fingers crossed up until now. As my old Irish father-in-law used to say, "A liar you can never trust!"

Actually, we are *not* too expensive. Well your customer thinks you *are* and **Rule Number 1** of business is: "the customer is *always right*". **Rule Number 2** is: "when the customer is wrong … see **Rule Number 1**." You are not there to prove that you are right. You are there to get some business. Who is *right* is immaterial! What the customer thinks is right is the ONLY thing that matters.

First I think you should know some history of our company [10 minutes "blah"] … and that's how we got where we are today. This is the 21st century. Nobody cares, about your roots, your history, your founder or when you were "established". It is not interesting to 99% of your customers. And there's only a 1:100 chance the other 1% are interested (and I bet this customer isn't in that 1%). The most *un*-persuasive words in the world are "I" and "we". The most persuasive word is "YOU" … and your only interest (YOU the customer) is what I (the seller) can DO for YOU today, tomorrow and beyond.

We'll come back to your point later if we may. But first I want Bob to show you a PowerPoint presentation of all the things our company does. Leave the laptop at home ... LEAVE THE LAPTOP AT HOME! A boilerplate standard PowerPoint presentation is a sales killer. It is "Death by PowerPoint". An instant sales demolisher. *Ask any customer.* It is a crutch for rotten sales people. You cannot begin selling until you know what the customer wants to buy and right now you don't ... all the other stuff about your company is irrelevant.

Well that's a very interesting proposal. However let me tell you what *we* were thinking on our way to see you this morning. It is a fact of human nature that other people (your customers!) are least open to any of your proposals if they have just presented one of their own. If you respond to any of your customer's ideas (however stupid) with little or no consideration or discussion but with an instant alternative proposal of your own, you might just as well have said, "Yeah, yeah, yeah ... and all that! Now here's *my* really brilliant idea". Like it or not your customers prefer the sound of their own voice just as much as you prefer the sound of yours.

Yes. If I can just stop you there. I think I know what you're going to say so let me tell you how we can address this type of issue you are probably experiencing. You don't know you idiot! You really DON'T know what they are going to say! In my time as a chronic interrupter I have wrongly assumed a customer was about to complain about my product's price, its "ease of use", its weight and its "suitability for purpose". Each time I have interrupted in this way I have answered a question that hadn't even been asked and thereby introduced a big unnecessary question mark in the customer's mind. So many people are prone to this bad habit. Instead of listening most amateur persuaders are just waiting for their turn to talk!

Telling isn't selling

Here's a question for you: You're telling somebody something; it is a very interesting thing (at least you think it is). So how long (on average) is it before the other normal person drifts off, falls asleep or starts thinking about something else? Is it 15 minutes, 10 minutes, 5 minutes, 3 minutes, 1 minute or 30 seconds?

They may be nodding, smiling, looking at you, saying "mmm ... mmm", but at what "time-point" has this target person (often your customer) usually lost the thread of what you're saying? Have a think about this for a moment ...

Right and your answer is? ... 3 minutes? ... 1 minute? You will be much closer to the truth, for the vast majority of the human race, if you settle on *30 seconds*! They may drift back to you every so often but they will drift away again in no time at all.

Human brains get bored quickly ... very quickly. If you ask someone to concentrate on one thought or one object and nothing else for as long as they can, they will, generally, find it very difficult. Try it yourself by performing this exercise right now (it's a pretty standard introductory exercise for people who are learning to meditate). Go and get an egg from your kitchen and place it on a table in front of you ... fix it somehow in a little pile of salt so that it doesn't roll off.

Make sure you also have a wristwatch or a clock next to you with a second hand.

Sit down, on a chair in front of the egg. Now make sure that there is little chance of anyone interrupting you for the next ten minutes. Start timing. Stare at your egg – remove ALL other thoughts from your mind – notice only its shape … its colour … its texture … its size … let no other thought enter your mind … consider only your egg.

Concentrate only on your egg … the instant any thought (a cup of coffee, dry cleaning, sex, the hardness of the chair you're sitting on, thinking about the effort of thinking about the egg and so on) other than a thought about your egg enters your mind, STOP … look at the second hand. Now … how much time has passed since you started? I will be extremely surprised if more than a few seconds has passed … you will be very lucky to get to 30 seconds!

Telling people about all your stuff is a very poor way of persuading them because (as you can see) most of us just can't concentrate for long enough. So most people (your customers) only hear the first three or four words of what you're saying before they start formulating what they are going to say back to you! Awful isn't it? They just don't listen. So what can you do? Actually the answer is "lots" and it's not that difficult.

First you can remember that there is little new under the sun and take advice from the famous 17th century scientist, Isaac Newton (whose work included defining the law of gravity) and his *Philosophiae Naturalis Principia Mathematica* (1687). And within that magnum opus his Third Law of Motion which briefly stated that: "every action has an equal and opposite reaction".

Equal and opposite reaction

As my dairy-farming brother-in-law says, "Cows don't give milk. You have to take it from them." And this most definitely applies to selling. No customer on earth just hands you a sale. You (the seller) must go in there and pull it out for yourself. But how you do this is not at all intuitive. The natural tendency of most amateur sellers is to try to push the sale out on a black tide of well intentioned "pitch". And classic "sales pitches" rarely work. The more push felt by the customer the more the customer will push back to maintain the balance. If your customer ever laughs to break the pressure he's feeling and tells you that you are, "a great salesperson" you need to get worried! As Newton told us three hundred years ago, the equal and opposite reaction mechanism is going on inside your customer's head and in this case the result will be to shut you out.

> Socrates was a man who went around giving people advice ... so they killed him.
>
> FROM AN ESSAY ON THE HISTORY OF THE WORLD
> BY AN 11-YEAR-OLD CHILD

And just as with "milking a cow" which is an operation requiring a delicate touch, so it is with selling. Your customer won't (unlike a cow) kick you if you get it wrong. But you are still faced with the fact that the more you push ... the more the ~~cow~~ customer, will push back and you'll get nothing.

Why is this?

Well, as American President Harry S. Truman said many years ago, "The best way to give advice to your children is

to find out what they want and then advise them to do it."
None of us likes to be told what to do (and where children
are concerned this is particularly relevant). I mean, just
imagine going to see your doctor who doesn't listen to your
problem but gives you the same diagnosis and treatment
he gave to a patient he saw a few weeks ago. The only reason he does this is that the treatment worked for the other
patient.

If *you* don't listen, if *you* are not initially inquisitive, if *you* do
not clarify the explicit problems experienced by THIS
customer – the one you are sitting in front of now – you will
be perceived as disinterested, self centred and totally idiotic.
You, a total innocent Amateur Salesperson (senior executive
notwithstanding) are actually perpetuating the stereotype
image of an average pushy salesperson.

Breathing your own CO_2

So ... if I am saying that you can't *tell* your prospects and
customers all about your products, ideas and services what
can you do to *sell* them? You start by understanding how not
to "un-sell".

Nature, as we know, "abhors a vacuum", but human beings
loathe dead air.

Therefore when there is a silence in a room most untrained
sellers become very anxious. They talk about anything to fill
the space. And as the thing they know best is their own
product, they yap some more about all of its features, ele-
ments, advantages and virtues. They cover, over and over
again, the material dealt with just a few minutes before. The

selling-air becomes re-breathed CO_2 – the leftover product of respiration. Carbon dioxide (CO_2) is actually used in hospitals to get patients to breathe again once their lungs have stopped working. Because it is the presence of CO_2 in our lungs that makes us take another breath.

If as a school child you ever tried that highly dangerous experiment of breathing the same air in and out of a plastic bag (NO DON'T DO IT you're too sensible now!) you will have found that after a few cycles your breathing becomes faster and faster as your lungs become desperate for oxygen which is in increasingly short supply in the gas in the bag. You very rapidly start to hyperventilate. The same happens to your persuasive powers when you yap too much in front of your customers.

Stories abound in the bars and cafes of most major cities where sales people "hang-out", about the pure hell of visiting a top client accompanied by the boss or other non-sales colleague. The punch-line is usually the same one and goes something like this: "And having told me, before we went out that they would let *me* do all the talking, when we got there they wouldn't shut-up!" (Don't believe me? Ask one of your sales people who you can trust for an honest answer.)

Alas, the more a seller talks, the more the un-selling process is taking place. You will see your prospect's eyes losing focus. You will see the occasional flick-gaze over your shoulder. You will notice the momentary interest in a rough fingernail. Subconsciously the heels are digging-in! Your customer doesn't want to be talked at or pushed and neither do YOU when you're a customer. You and your product, service or idea are not a "special case". The laws of persuasion apply just as much when the boot is on the other foot. Just like YOU, your customer wants to be understood.

> We have two ears and one tongue so that we would listen more and talk less.
>
> DIOGENES: ANCIENT GREEK PHILOSOPHER

And as very basic as this advice is, **not talking** is usually very hard to do if you're an enthusiastic, passionate but untrained seller.

The great riddle in selling is this: you cannot sell if you don't have a relationship. And you cannot have a relationship unless you have sold and proved the value of your proposition. You might be thinking to yourself that this type of approach only works in individual, one-to-one, simple-selling (cars, refrigerators, cleaning services and so on) and not when endeavouring to close large-scale complex sales with huge corporate accounts. It is my tough duty to tell you that you are wrong.

It actually doesn't matter how complicated the sale is (international software contract, an order for 20 jumbo-jet airliners, a global financial information system), you are not dealing with an anonymous grey corporate bulk, you are dealing with people. And these people are making decisions and they are dead-scared of getting it wrong. They have just the same emotions as you do: they are ambitious to do better, they are afraid of failing, they have no idea what is going to happen next and they are really confused with uncertainty.

To cap it all – just like you and most humans – they are play-ing the same unhelpful record over and over again in their head:

> "What will *they* do when they discover I'm
> only me?"

All humans have a great need to feel good about themselves. If you ask most senior executives how they are feeling they'll say, "Oh me? Fine!" But as an American business associate told me recently the word "FINE" actually stands for:

> **F****ked-up
>
> **I**nsecure
>
> **N**eurotic and
>
> **E**motional

I recently asked a senior executive (who was as usual seeking some persuasive behavioural "pointers" prior to an import-ant client meeting) what his primary goal was whenever he met an important customer and he replied, "I always try to impress them!" Fine!

About 25 years ago I worked for a large company in which the main board directors liked to hold regular key-customer-lunches for which we, the members of the sales-force, were required to supply the lunchtime guests. At one of these lunches our "guests" (customers) were four, self-made entre-preneurs with a very successful global business. These men spent several tens of millions of dollars a year with my com-pany. They were not either academics or particularly "well-read" and I doubt they had ever been to university or college. Their main chat was about sport, (football, golf, cricket, etc) a landscape in which the director/host on this occasion was completely lost. Instead of getting the gentlemen to tell him all they knew about sport (their chosen subject), he rapidly turned the conversation round to the current London theatre scene ... an area in which he was an *intellectual expert* and they were at-sea.

"Tell me," he asked. "What do you think about [George Bernard] Shaw's play *Arms and the Man* at the National? I'm thinking in particular about the characterizations of the two key players Raina and Catherine?" The lunch terminated rapidly. Afterwards the director came up to me beaming as if the lunch had been a total success, "Huh! You've got to *show* those sort of guys haven't you!?" he said.

The next day one of them called me and asked: "Is that director of yours really bright or is he actually an idiot?" Next year we lost the business and didn't get it back for another fifteen years.

If you think this is all New Age feel-my-pain, emotional nonsense and you're seeking some down-to-earth brass-tacks, old fashioned guidance in selling and persuading, there's a yellowing, faded book you might take a glance at which will back-up what you're reading here. Way back, before the Second World War, a man called Dale Carnegie published a book in the USA entitled *How to Win Friends and Influence People*. Actually it is far from "yellowing" and "faded" and is still in print today (30 million copies worldwide) but I'm always amazed at how few people in business have read it. In HTWFAIP, over 70 years on from its original publication date, you will find this same accurate guidance into the quirks of human behaviour. The whole book is set down in rather old-fashioned language but it's all there.

Following are just ten headings taken from Dale Carnegie's summary of his own book. My simple definitions are tacked on below. All of these techniques are covered in detail in this little book you are holding in your hand. With the insights provided by modern behavioural psychology you will soon have a powerful understanding of the simple ways your customers can be persuaded to buy from you.

1. **Ask questions instead of giving direct instructions.**
   When a person is talking they feel more in charge of the situation. (Just like you do.)

2. **Be a good listener. Encourage others to talk about themselves.**
   People actually don't care much about YOU … they care about themselves. (Just like you do.)

3. **Let the other person do the talking.**
   Human beings like the sound of their own voice more than yours. (Just like you do.)

4. **Talk in the terms of the other man's interest.**
   People aren't against you they are for themselves. (Just like you are.)

5. **Make the other person feel important and do it sincerely.**
   People who feel good about themselves produce good results. (This includes giving you more business.)

6. Let the other person feel the idea is his/hers.

You are not there to "impress" you are there to get business. (Who cares whose idea it was? They do ... just like you.)

7. Show respect for the other person's opinions. Never tell someone they are wrong.

Business Rule Number 1: the customer is *always* right. Business rule Number 2: when the customer is wrong, see Business Rule Number 1.

8. Talk about your own mistakes first.

"I'm sorry I was wrong" are amongst the rarest but most powerful words in business. (Everybody finds them difficult to say – just like you.)

9. Sympathize with the other person.

Sympathy for problems rates among the top five requirements for customer satisfaction. (Your customers have problems and want to be heard, at length – just like you.)

10. Start with questions the other person will answer yes to.

"Yes framing" or the "Law of Consistency" is deeply imbedded in our human psyche. If you can get a customer saying "Yes" to a series of simple questions, then they are 80% more likely to say, "Yes" to your more difficult questions later. (Ask any child ... especially your own.)

To influence: get the other person talking

There's a famous story of a young woman who dined with William Gladstone one evening, and with Benjamin Disraeli the next. (Gladstone and Disraeli were prominent British statesmen of the 19th century. They were bitter rivals.) Asked her impression of these two powerful men, the young woman replied, "When I left the dining room after sitting next to Mr. Gladstone, I thought he was the cleverest man in England. But after sitting next to Mr. Disraeli, I thought I was the cleverest woman in England."

DALE CARNEGIE: *HOW TO WIN FRIENDS AND INFLUENCE PEOPLE*
(1936)

The one thing I always recall from the HTWFAIP book is what Carnegie said about the word "I". During the 1920s when there were no automatic telephone exchanges in New York and all calls had to be routed through a human telephone operator, they carried out a survey to find the most often used word in the English language. After several months they discovered that word was, "I". It was used five times more often than any other word and yet, when tested by university researchers, it was found that this was the most *unpersuasive* word in the world.

Further research revealed that, at the other end of the scale, the most persuasive word was no more used than any other word. It was not "sex" or "win" or "free" or "easy" (which all rank quite high on the persuasive list). No, the most *persuasive* word of all was back then, and still is: "*YOU*".

People, (your customers, your staff, your friends and your colleagues) care most of all about themselves. And if they feel that you genuinely care about them and their interests they will give you more business. If you give them your ear and stop talking they will be impressed. If you stop trying to impress them and let them speak they will be charmed. If you stop trying to charm them with your brilliance and make them feel important they will give you more than you ever imagined.

Summary

The simple message of this chapter? *Never miss a good opportunity to* SHUT UP.

2

Never make a statement when you could ask a question

> **Quizmaster:** Can you complete this well known
> children's nursery rhyme: Old MacDonald
> had a—
>
> **Contestant:** [thinks] ...farm!
>
> **Quizmaster:** Correct! And for an extra ten points can
> you spell it?
>
> **Contestant:** Yes! E I E I O!

It's a funny old world. You don't always get the answers you were expecting.

You'd have thought (wouldn't you?) that in order to sell your product service or idea, you have to say lots of things about it? The "gift of the gab", "fast talking" and "smooth tongued rascal" are all epithets used to describe the verbal manner of persuasive rogues and the ubiquitous "used car salesman". The sort of people you might encounter in a sales setting but come away from meeting feeling that you've just been "had".

If that's your view I have bad news and worse news for you. The bad news is that fast-talking does work. The worse news is that if you ever use it to sell "once", that customer will never want to buy from you again.

If you have ever witnessed this "yap" method of selling work successfully on unsuspecting "innocents" you will know it is quite an eye-opener!

In 2007 successful fast-talking-persuasion was actually demonstrated, on British TV, by the brilliant young illusionist Derren Brown. He was filmed, shopping in New York, using a specially devised *fast-talk* script which enabled him to distract shopkeepers whilst he paid for expensive jewellry and classy wristwatches with blank pieces of paper! And not just once.

He did it, brazenly, over and over again, in different shops, using only $50-bill-sized sheets and (literally) a lot of fast talking! Interestingly, the only person he didn't fool was a humble hot-dog seller. (For the avoidance of any doubt I have to tell you that he returned all the items afterwards.)

The blank sheets were not hidden in a wad with a real note on the top and bottom; they were right there for all to see … including the shopkeeper.

Using a hidden camera, set up across the street, Brown was filmed entering a typical, up-market Fifth Avenue store, posing as a genuine customer. Having asked the assistant to show him an expensive piece of merchandise he said, after due consideration, that he would like to buy it for cash …

around $1000. From his wallet he produced the wad of blank paper and peeled each "bill" into the assistant's hand. As he did so he distracted the assistant with a series of simple questions and statements.

"By the way is there a subway station near here?" [50, 100, 150 ... keeps counting the "money" out]

"Yes."

"Is it on the next street or is it further?" [250, 300, 350 more sheets of blank paper]

"It's just over there."

"I see so I cross over the road and walk a couple of blocks." [450, 500, 550 ... keeps counting the "notes"]

"Yes."

"I find it so confusing in this city ... [keeps counting the paper] I've never been to New York before I could do with a coffee too ... is there a Starbucks close by? [750, 800 ... looks out of the window] ... ah yes there's one over there. [900, 950, 1000] Right well thank you very much!"

Brown picked up the merchandise without hesitation and walked out of the store. [The camera cuts back to a stunned shop assistant looking down at his handful of worthless paper and suddenly rushing to the door... Alas the "thief" had long gone.]

It is astonishingly easy to confuse and distract a human brain but such fast talking isn't what true selling is all about.

True selling is about persuasion. And the fact is we rarely persuade anyone to do anything: people (your customers) persuade themselves. "Statements" and "telling" are very *inefficient* true selling tools.

"Questions", on the other hand, are the salesperson's most persuasive weapon. And the good thing about "questions" (chatty conversational questions) is that you can use them time and time again on the same prospective customer and sell more each time.

Why *questions* are the basic tools of successful selling

Questions and answers combined create a dialogue and (as you learnt in Chapter 1) a dialogue is much more effective than a classic sales pitch (i.e. You making statements and putting them to sleep).

If you fail to get this dialogue underway, *with the customer doing at least 60% of the talking,* you will rarely secure an order, contract or sale for your business. Your questions (and the way you answer the questions put to you by your customer) are the most important parts of your sales discussion.

As an **Amateur Seller** (I'm not being patronizing but I think that's why you bought this book) you are strongly recommended (by me) to get into the habit of preparing your questions in advance and asking them in the right order. And even if you are only sitting there watching your company's professional sales executive at work then at least you will understand why they're doing what they're doing and keep quiet. (After all, *you* don't want to be the nightmare colleague they talk about afterwards who wouldn't shut up.)

I once worked for Rank Xerox, the business machine company in the UK, and I still keep an unsigned contract for a large copying machine in my filing cabinet. This piece of paper is now over 35 years old but I hold on to it for nostalgic reasons. And actually it was part of the inspiration for this book.

In the "signature box" of the contract there is no signature but there on the left-hand side is a small blue ink mark about 2 mm long. It was where a prospective customer placed his pen on the paper to sign and my boss's boss (the area manager and not a trained seller) who was with me for the day suddenly said, "Oh ... and there's something else we need to tell you. You will need to get a much larger power supply for this upgraded machine and we will have to bring in a crane to load it in from the road."

These two items were true but would cost the customer nothing (all part of the service) ... but he took his pen off the paper. The spell was broken. We then spent half an hour discussing whether the upgraded printing machine was actually worth all the trouble and hassle after all. He said he would need to think about it and let us know. He never did.

But how many non sales executives, senior managers and company directors actually appreciate the real importance of questions? Has anybody demonstrated to them why, psychologically, questions are more persuasive than statements or pitching? Why do they stick doggedly to their boiler-plate presentations. Here are a few reasons:

Lack of confidence: many senior executives are great managers and political animals. They know what their company does or makes but have little real understanding of why the customers are buying the products and what they are doing with them. (I was once at a Sales Conference internal "Fun Quiz" during which the CEO at the time answered over half the questions about the company's products, incorrectly.) Subsequently such senior people don't want to be exposed or get into an argument with real customers.

They suffer from corporate myopia: they are so in love with their own company that they fail to appreciate that the customer loves his own company more. Phrases that typically begin, "You really must appreciate our position here ..." are a dead give away! Your customer will do nothing for YOU until YOU have done everything for them. And to be able to do that you must listen to what they want.

So much of successful "communication" is about listening!

And it is one of the most important everyday tasks which amateur sellers need to get used to. In selling you are not simply waiting for your turn to talk. As my brother always reminds me, *effective communication* is not like the average Etherington family party ... usually a noisy affair ... in which everybody is talking and nobody's listening.

Humans all communicate as a reaction to various stimuli in our immediate environment. The psychologist Abraham

Maslow defined what he called "a hierarchy of needs" which shows exactly how basic human needs are organized. The needs which he illustrated are universal, as is the need to communicate. In order to establish the needs and desires of others, we must communicate. And that means that we must listen.

But there's something else too ... Most people who have ever attended a professional sales training programme in the past 20 years will know that the secret of success lies in the skill of asking the right questions and then listening ... really listening ... to the answer. However very few of these training programmes ever explain the whole truth to the delegates about why questions are so powerful.

They will have been told that questions bring them both information and understanding about the things that are important to the prospective customer. And this is quite true but it is only part of the answer.

The other very interesting (and in some ways more powerful) fact is the way a question focuses the mind of the person being questioned. You have heard the expression "I can only do one thing at a time" or the criticism levelled at most men that they are not "multitasking"? Well when somebody (anybody) is concentrating on answering a question that is very true.

When you ask someone a "conversational" question they are pretty well forced to think about what you want them to think about. Without them realizing it, you mentally get hold of their jacket at points "X" and "Y" and ...

jerk them towards you! (and they feel *nothing*!)

It is almost impossible for a questioned person to think about anything else but the answer to your question. On the other hand while the average amateur seller is making the standard boiler-plate pitch, their customer can easily think of other things especially 101 reasons why they do NOT need your product or service.

Questions are powerful because the right ones enable you to control the thinking of your customers.

So starting with the "power of control" here are the top 10 reasons for asking questions:

Understand the vital nature of information

1. You grab and hold your customer's attention.
Your questions give your customer the chance to speak.

And a person who is speaking cannot let their thoughts wander without you seeing it.

2. **You force your customer to think about what YOU want them to think about.** And what you want the customer to think about is the problem or challenge he has that your solution can fix.

3. **You get instant feedback from sudden changes in your customer's Body Language and Voice Tone.** Because these are so difficult to control consciously, they are the most telling of all the aspects of human communication.

Keep control of the conversation

4. **You vacuum up information about your customer's situation,** problems, desires, understanding and opinions. You cannot make a sale unless you find out what the customer wants to buy. Your customers do things for their reasons not yours.

5. **You pick the subject(s) to be discussed.** As we know from watching combative political discussions on modern TV stations, the person who asks the questions leads the way. Your objective (with your chatty questions) is to make the customer let you have their thoughts and feelings on the points you believe need to be discussed thereby placing control of the discussion in your hands.

6. **You demonstrate your interest in the customer and their issues.** In doing this simple thing you also remind yourself not to "pitch" because the only thing the customer is interested in is *their* problems not your *stuff*.

Move from "supplier" to "trusted advisor"

7. You attract the customer's confidence. Your questions have the immediate effect of raising the self esteem of the person being questioned. This is because your honest enquiry about their thoughts and opinions demonstrates respect for their views. All the people on the earth (including you and me) value what they say more than what they hear.

8. You generate thinking time. While the customer is composing the answer to your question YOU have time to strategize in your own head. Your customer has no script so don't be surprised if things don't go to plan.

> I know that you believe that you understood what you think I said, but I am not sure you realize that what you heard is not what I meant.
>
> ROBERT MCCLOSKEY
> U.S. STATE DEPARTMENT SPOKESMAN IN 1984
> (OFTEN ATTRIBUTED INCORRECTLY TO
> PRESIDENT RICHARD NIXON)

Minimize errors in understanding

9. You paraphrase what you believe you have just heard. Your customer's answers reveal background, market conditions, worries and expectations. Their tone of voice, manner of speaking and body language, are all "tells" revealing things they do not say. (Human communication is 55% body language, 38% voice tone and 7% content.)

10. **You lessen the danger of your saying something daft or contradictory** because the risk is transferred to the customer. (Old saying: God gave us two ears and one mouth and we should use them in that same ratio.) If you are listening properly, you can't simultaneously, say anything daft. And you reduce the risk of aggravating any differences of opinion between you and your customer. Statements (by you) harden and provoke reaction (the so-called "Defend and Attack" spiral) whereas "chatty questions" encourage relaxation, reduce cross-table tension and encourage reconciliation.

Questions are your primary sales tool and it is therefore very important that you learn to become skilful in asking them as soon as you can.

So, to *sell*, stop talking and start asking questions

In his classic novella *Animal Farm*, about a failed "communist" revolution, author George Orwell famously said, "All animals are equal but some animals are more equal than others".

Alas it isn't quite so with questions; although in general a question is nearly always better than a statement, they are not all "equal". For example, some questions of a bland and interrogative nature, can actually wreck a sale if you ask too many. And most amateur salespeople DO ask too many of these simply because they're "easy"; no preparation required!

Other questions, carefully thought about and prepared in advance by successful professional sellers, are felt by customers on the receiving end to demonstrate much more interest in the problems the customer would like to be fixed.

So it is worth looking at the types of question – good and bad – which you could use and how, when (and if) you should use any of them. All the most popular modern selling models taught to professional sales people, from Huthwaite Inc's **SPIN Selling**™ to Achieve Global's **PSS**™ (**P**rofessional **S**elling **S**kills), use questions as the basic tool. So we don't need to set our focus on any particular approach; they all boil down to the same thing.

Types of question

The direct question

A favourite of the more aggressive TV political interviewers: "Tell me Prime Minister how much is the public finance overspend?"

In the selling world it sounds more like: "How soon do you need to make this decision, Mr. Prospect?" "Who is the person who will make the final decision?"

The indirect question

These appear more like statements but are actually questions in disguise. They are particularly useful when dealing with people who are, clearly, keen to impress you: "I am particularly interested to discover which sales executives, in your opinion, are likely to fail."

The real question

(One that requires an answer): "What are you going to do?"

The leading question

Often used by experienced sales executives to "close" a sale and get an order or contract: " So you'll send me the contract by Monday ... Yes?" "Could you put me through to Mr. Prospect please ... thank you?"

The rhetorical question

The question is asked and answered by the questioner: "Is there any reason to provide extra spares? They are easily available on the High Street."

The open question

These are the sort of questions used by journalists containing the words "What? When? Why? Where? How? Who?" that can't be answered with a simple "Yes" or "No". Many (most) sales training programmes make a big fuss about the need for sales people to ask these all the time. The reason (they say) is that they get the customer to open up. Yet there is actually not one shred of evidence that they accelerate a sale. It is simply folklore. Just getting a prospect *talking* isn't half as powerful as getting them to tell you about their problems (the ones you can fix). And you can do that with Open and Closed questions (but more of that later).

Open questions would typically be: "*How* do you deal with the normal run of defects?" "*Where* do you currently source your financial data from?"

The closed question

This is the opposite to the above. They can be answered with a "Yes" or "No" and provided they have been correctly prepared in advance can be part of a very persuasive persuaders tool kit: "Can you tell me about the biggest problem you have here?" "Is the lack of automatic data supply causing you any issues?"

The alternative question

This type of question is very effective for giving a prospective customer the perception that they have a choice, yet both answers give the questioner a reply which favours the questioner. True the customer could, when offered the alternative, say "neither suits me" but you'd be surprised how often (80% of the time in fact) they take one of your alternatives: "When would be a good day for our next meeting Tuesday 24th or Friday 3rd?" "When you consider the scope of this proposal would you like it to cover the world or just Europe? It's really your choice."

So these are all the basic question types. But sales is a "process" in which you have to hold the hand of a customer and lead them (with your questions) towards the conclusion you want. Randomly asking any old questions will get you into trouble quickly ... rather like getting "the bends" if you surface too fast from the depths of the ocean!

Here's why:

Get the sale ... not "the bends"

The context in which various questions are used is important. Most amateur sellers are in big hurry to tell the customer all about their stuff. Yes they've been on courses ... or read a book or two, like this one. (Must ask questions.) So they quickly go through the ritual of a few questions (like the book said) and then – quick as a flash – go into the pitch; they can't wait!

If you tend to do this you're behaving like a deep-sea diver who is making his way too swiftly to the surface. Any diver who ascends from the depths of the ocean at too fast a pace, places a massive strain on his pulmonary system. This strain manifests itself through the formation of tiny nitrogen bubbles in his bloodstream. These give rise to massive painful cramps known as "*the bends*" which if left untreated can easily and rapidly lead to death!

In a similar fashion, when an Amateur Seller produces his solution too early in the sales process it also triggers a chain reaction which usually ends with the early death of the sale. Because, by seeking to get to the oxygen of his solution as fast as possible, he finds that he encounters price objections ("the bends") very early on.

Most average Amateur Sales attempts fail because the sellers have no idea of the damage done to a sale by their own indecent haste to present their solution.

This can be seen more clearly if we compare the length of time Average and Professional Sellers spend on each phase of the process.

The time-line of an *average price-oriented sale looks like this:*

Average amateur sale

On the other hand research shows that a well conducted and truly successful sale usually has a much longer investigation phase (questions). Subsequently there is much less need for price negotiations and price discounting at the end. Indeed, all the research shows that the longer spent on the "investigative" or anticipation phase – just like birthdays, Christmas, foreplay – the stronger the effect of the ultimate event.

Top professional sale

If you're an academic ...

I need to get into a bit of "dry" stuff now, so if the "how" rather than the "why" of the *mechanics of questions as persuasive equipment* is more important to you, just at the moment, you can skip forward to Chapter 3 (immediately) then come back here later. Chapter 3 sets out the most persuasive four-step questioning model I know: **"SWOT"***

So what do you want to do? Skip forward? OK, off you go then ... see you back here later.

Welcome back.

The current conditions, client set-up and situation determine the content of your questions. So you need to identify the situation you find the customer in and then use appropriate questions to suit.

Each question you ask your customer will have a classification. It will either be a *lone question*, a *linked question* (which will be part of a series of questions – see Chapter 3) or a *reply question* (which is often used by professional sales people instead of a direct reply to avoid prematurely "putting-their-foot-in-it").

Once you (the seller) have correctly identified the class of question appropriate to the situation you find yourself in, you will then be able to find the right place to ask the question during the discussion or conversation.

---

*(Laboriously developed, over 30 years, in the "school of hard knocks" by me. Lovingly passed on to you for just the price of this book.)

The eight laws of questioning

Whilst *asking a question* probably appears to be an extremely basic exercise with little or no built-in difficulty, asking the wrong type at the wrong moment (usually too early) in the sales process, can actually make a sale *less* likely. Yes, a question is generally preferable to a statement but being able to finesse your questions correctly will place you a million miles ahead of most other Amateur Persuaders ... I am going to show you how to do it.

OK? Here goes ... Every time you ask a question you need to bear in mind that there are **eight basic rules** which control the art and science of asking persuasive questions. By sticking to these rules you will increase the likelihood of successfully getting your customer to persuade himself. So keep the following in mind when you prepare any questions for use at your next client meeting. (Yes you *must always prepare* ... it will **not** "be alright on the night".)

1. Keep it short. Keep away from meandering questions because they are far harder for your prospect to answer. Clarify the reason for the question if you need to but don't go on and on. For example, the following is OK: "So that we can calculate the right numbers for you, can you tell me how many of your staff will require the full programme and how many the compact version?"

And it is always recommended that you explain, initially, the reason you are asking questions. Most customers expect you to pitch at them anyway and it can be a shock when you start asking them quite a few things instead. So give a bit of warning such as: "So that I can give you only the information you're looking for and avoid wasting your time, I would like to ask you a few questions to ascertain whether or not we can assist you in this case."

Some very interesting research carried out at Arizona State University in the past few years proves that if you give another person a reason – almost any reason will do it seems – for complying with any request you are making, they are 80% more likely to comply.

There is also a very efficient three step opening statement which will reduce your need to explain that you are going to be *asking* more than *telling* during the rest of the meeting with this customer. I call it, **The Three Rs** and if you're ever stuck with what to say at the start then I recommend you too open with:

Reason

Route

Result

I remind them of the *Reason* for the meeting. I tell them the *Route* I am going to take (asking questions). I tell them what the *Result* will be (no "wants" uncovered = I leave; worries revealed = I stay to discuss further.) So if I ever come to see you in your business you'll generally hear me open like this:

"Mr. Prospect what I'd like to do today is ascertain whether we at SpokenWord can offer you the type of Negotiation training programme you're looking for at Acme. [**R**eason] In order to do that I'd like to ask you some questions about your business. [**R**oute] It will quickly become very clear to both of us, from your answers, if SpokenWord can help you. If we can I will stay and learn more about your requirements and if not I'll go ... is that OK with you?" [**R**esult]

2. Be understood. "Could you describe for me the pedagogical criteria by which you will judge the success of any intranet/extranet project, how you will measure those criteria and what your time scales are?"

This *amateur* sales person is clearly more intent on impressing the prospective customer with a few complex words which the customer might not be familiar with. But this will generally have the effect of making the customer feel mistrustful and unsure. You are there to *sell* ... NOT to *impress.* Only use your own buzzwords and technical terms if the person you are sitting in front of at the moment has shown that they know them by using them too. It would not be difficult to rephrase the question: "Could you tell me what you would like this new IT project to do for your business and how soon you need to complete it?"

3. Be accurate. You need to ask precise questions because if you do not you will get wandering waffling answers. "How do you see prices in the UK commercial property market going in the near to medium future?" and "What do think about the merger between Reuters and Thomson Financial?" are not at all precise. So rephrase in a precise and accurate manner: "Do you think that commercial property prices in London will go up or down in the next two years?" and "What main benefit do you think the customers of Reuters and Thomson will gain from the merger?"

There are a few exceptions to this. For example when a quiet, non-talkative customer needs to be encouraged to open up a bit. A more general, "what's your opinion?" "what do you think?" question can get their tongue loosened quite quickly.

4. **Keep it simple.** "How much training do your sales people get each year and how good are they subsequently at opening a call, closing a call, overcoming objections and negotiating?" This question has five parts and five part questions (or actually any question with more than *one* part) will have many quite different answers. Your customer will get confused. He may have to think about the (input) training/coaching activities of the sales managers and trainers and simultaneously about the (output) results of the training provided. So ask separate questions: "How much training do you offer your sales force each year?" Then when you have a clear answer you can ask the next part: "How good are they at opening the sales process?" and so on until you have the precise information you need.

5. **Tell them what's coming.** There is an interesting study that shows top (successful) sellers often tell the other side that a question is coming by hanging a big label on it: "HERE COMES A QUESTION". It sounds something like this: "Mr. Prospect I'd like to ask you a question at this point and it is this ... how often each week does your existing system breakdown?" Constructing a question like this has the psychological effect of concentrating the questioned person's thoughts before you even ask the actual question.

6. **Determine to be persistent.** You need to know how much tile adhesive your prospective customer buys each

month from your competitors. They have asked you to quote for the project but won't give you a precise answer on current quantity on which you can base your calculation. Don't give up but continue in a roundabout way: "How many tiles have to be laid, in total on this site?" A short while later: "How large are the tiles you are using?" Eventually: "What quantity of adhesive do you estimate per square metre?" You now have enough information to punch in to your calculator to give you what you need to know.

Persistence

Nothing in the world can take the place of persistence. Talent will not; nothing is more common than unsuccessful men with talent. Genius will not; unrewarded genius is almost a proverb. Education will not; the world is full of educated derelicts. Persistence and determination alone are omnipotent.

SIGN ON THE OFFICE WALL OF RAY KROC
FOUNDER OF MCDONALDS
(ORIGINALLY ATTRIBUTED TO US PRESIDENT
CALVIN COOLIDGE)

---

7. **Keep horses to courses.** You must stick to questions that the particular customer you're sitting in front of can answer. As stated previously in this chapter, you are not there to *impress* the person ... you're there to *sell*. Don't ask an accountant technical details about a product and don't ask an engineer to explain the method of calculating profit. (I have even seen amateur sellers try to sell sophisticated office equipment to a receptionist!)

If you do ask a senior person for technical details they will generally hate to tell you they don't know and will often start to make things up to cover the absence of knowledge. They will also start to feel less sure of themselves and the result of that will be less probability that they will give you a sale. You must return quickly to the prospective customer's area of direct experience if the answers you are getting are beginning to sound woolly.

8. **Be clear.** I am regularly called on the phone by Amateur Sellers who would like to do business with us but speak so fast that I just don't get it. Whether you're speaking to customers face-to-face or on the telephone you must speak slowly. You must speak up and enunciate each word of your questions clearly. By showing the customer that your question is important and that you are not just dumping your words on them, your customer will in turn provide you with a serious answer. And give the person the chance to reply … most amateur sellers listen to just the opening few words of a reply before they are already composing their response.

And do not (all too common fault) reply to your own question yourself just because you think you're going to get a reply you don't want to hear, or you are getting impatient, or even because you really want to impress this person with your own product or market knowledge.

> Terrible day isn't it? I don't suppose you're in the market for a product like mine are you? … No? … and not likely to be any time soon? … No, I didn't think you were but thanks anyway.
>
> ME, AS A YOUNG SALESMAN WAY BACK IN THE 1970s

The two essential things that questions do for you:

1. They provide you with information.
2. They get your customer thinking.

You cannot begin to sell until:

● You know what your customer might persuade himself to buy; and
● Until that customer wants what you can offer enough to buy it.

So leave that laptop firmly closed (or at home) at the start of the sale; this means YOU (however senior you are in the company).

Before you can do anything to match your customer's needs you must know what problem you are trying to address. Before you launch into your canned presentation which your laptop is calling you from your briefcase to present (let me out ... let me out!) you must know if you actually have a potential customer across the desk or if you are both simply wasting your time.

1. Establishing your customer's wants. It took me years to discover that it is no good trying to sell people what YOU think they NEED. People (customers) want what THEY WANT which is *not* always what they really need. Frustrating but true.

I once had a UK based managing director who instructed me (bellowed at me) that I should go out to America and tell those "Yanks" what they really needed to be buying. What he wanted me to sell was an international financial information product. What the American market wanted, on the other hand, was an equivalent domestic market product which we didn't have. The market may well have benefited greatly from the international product I had. But at that particular moment in history they did not believe they NEEDED it, so I sold very little. All the bellowing in the world wasn't going to change that.

If you are going to successfully identify this particular customer's explicit "wants", problems, worries or even to establish if they qualify as a customer, you must ask your questions in the following areas:

- The background and set-up in which the customer currently finds themselves.
- The "want", "worry", "headache", or "problem" your product or service can fix.
- The knock-on effects of not fixing the problem.
- The urgency of the desire to solve the problem.

In Chapter 3 you will be shown the "SWOT" model, a focused method of compiling and using all these questions but there are three main principals you need to pay attention to in all cases:

Principle 1

Your lead in must be light and innocuous in order to get the discussion underway. Your question must **not** exceed your customer's intellectual limits, make them suspicious or alarmed in any way. The classic sample question in the insurance business is not, "Let us suppose you were going to die tomorrow", but alternatively, "Let us suppose you had died yesterday".

So it is not, "How much do you make in each month on coffee and tea sales?" but "How many brands of coffee and tea do you have on your shelves?"

Principle 2

Don't let them know that you know secret confidential things about their business. If you have already discovered details of your customer's current situation background and set-up which you think he would regard as commercially sensitive or secret ("a little bird told me") – sales figures, senior resignation, purchase prices or production figures – then keep quiet!

You are not there to prove that you are great at international industrial espionage or have great insider contacts, you are there to sell; that's all. If it's on their website, has been in the press or on TV or is in their corporate brochure, fair enough. Apart from that *you know nothing*!

Principle 3

Do not make your customer feel interrogated with too many background questions. You should have done your homework well beforehand (not with the sales executive coming up in the lift five minutes ago) and these days much of what they want you to know is on their website anyway. Also if you appear to be seeking too much detailed information about their business your questions will make your prospective customer start to think of their own business as much more "highly complicated" than they had previously thought. If this happens then you will find it much more difficult to sell your product or service when the time is right. I know it is a pain to have to sit down and *prepare* so much and asking background questions as they occur to you is much easier than *preparing*, but you will do yourself no good if you fail here.

What the Professors found

An academic study conducted in the UK several years ago for an American based company showed that in an unsuccessful sale, almost twice as many so-called "background questions" were asked by Amateur Sellers (e.g. trainee sales executives, chief executives, engineers, technicians, accountants etc) compared with their more experienced top performing professional sales executives.

On the other hand only the top performing, regularly successful, Professional Sellers "dared" to ask questions about the possible negative knock-on effects of failing to address the problem, in order to develop the urgency of finding a solution.

---

2. **Do not use Leading Questions to identify problems you can fix.** Leading questions interpret problems from *your* point of view rather than your customer's and will not get you very far in selling. " I expect you find that your current gas boiler often breaks down, don't you?" "Errr ... no!" "Would you agree that a heavy copying machine is the last thing a company like yours needs?" "Well ours doesn't give us any trouble!"

So if you really want to identify and understand wants and worries from the customer's point of view then you must ask **Proper Questions**.

Proper Questions bring you: *information, reasons* (for the current problematic situation from the customer's standpoint) and control (so that you understand the prospective customer's situation correctly). Some Proper Questions might be:

"How high are current sales of your 'Focus' product?" [*Proper. Closed. Information.*]

"Why did you stop advertising on the internet?" [*Proper. Open. Reasons.*]

"So you're saying that the average training course takes two days?" [*Proper. Open. Reasons.*]

"Are you familiar with the recent Harvard Business School findings on this type of training? [*Proper. Closed. Catch Question. Are your competitors on the ball?*]

When you're getting ready for a customer visit you must prepare to ask this type of Proper Question with which you can develop their wants. It is best to write them in a notebook in "bullet" form so that you're not trying to remember them on the spot. I write mine in light pencil down the left hand page and use these "bullets" as the base to form the full questions which I compose during the meeting.

How to use questions to present your solution

The actual progress of any sale (helping the customer to talk about and think about the problem) towards the revelation of your solution, is covered in detail in Chapter 3. In a classic sale, the solution phase usually begins with the promise of a benefit:

"So from what we've discussed would you be interested if you could save 50 thousand, every year from now on?"

"Now I have a picture of the cost of failures would you like to cut your defects rate to .05%?"

"By cutting one aspect of your business process you could increase your profits between 25% and 95%. Would you like to know how?"

Now you know that ... you can generate more persuasive power

You will actually find it *even more powerful* to get the customer to express the benefits of introducing your solution or "benefit" *in their own words*:

"So if you had a solution to the problem we discussed, what type of annual savings would you see?"

"Supposing we had a solution that was able to get your defect rate down to .05% what difference would that make to your business?"

"If we could cut your rate of attrition by just 10% how much do you think your profits would increase?

Solutions are the only things your customer wants from you

Your products and services offer multiple benefits to your chosen market. These solutions (that's what *benefits* are) lie in the areas of safety, profit, image, simplification, flexibility and so on. The skill of top professional sales people rests in selecting the benefit which best matches the customer's "wants" or "predominant worry" or "nagging headache". This is usually obtained from the answer to the question leading into the presentation of your solution.

This is why you should avoid opening your "laptop presentation" before you fully understand the problem from your customer's point of view.

You will need to have made the choice of benefit you will show your customer in the preceding phase of clarifying wants. By saying "yes" to your lead-in question, your customer is asking for the presentation of your solution.

Control questions

What is known as your Control Question is the most important one you can ask as you go into your "benefit presentation". Throughout your sales meeting you need constantly to establish that your customer has understood what you have been explaining and showing them:

"Have I explained this clearly?"

"Have you understood the link between us and our American partners?"

"Can you identify the control system you'll use?"

It's the algebra lesson all over again

By the way, you can't count on your customer asking you to explain a point in more detail. People in general don't do that because they don't want to seem slow or "thick". Just like you in the algebra lesson at school years ago, they often hope that the point they don't understand will be revealed when you (the teacher) present your solution at the end. Also instead of asking your prospective customer: "Have you understood what I've been telling you?" you will find it more diplomatic to ask: "Have I expressed myself clearly?"

Know how powerful it is to link different types of question

You will find it very useful to sometimes link a presentation point with an information seeking question.

Information question:

"You'll receive the training in half-day modules. Do you see an advantage in that?"

First, your question makes your customer think about the argument in favour of your product.

Second, it makes your customers express the benefit from their point of view. Getting the customer to agree is a step towards closing your sale. Disagreement or "objections" reveal reservations in your customer's head which would have prevented a conclusion if they had remained undiscovered. But your previous questions (as opposed to the normal amateur "pitch") will actually help you avoid many normal sales objections and disagreements. This is because "questions" force the customer to think about and discuss problems they have which you can solve and that's all they're interested in.

It is often said that the "exception proves the rule", so it is worth noting that an Information Question, actually phrased as a Leading Question, becomes a Confirmation Question:

"I'm sure you agree that this approach greatly simplifies the process?"

"Don't you think that our software designer had a stroke of genius here?"

"The savings really show here, don't they?"

There are three important points which need to be made about this questioning technique:

1. You can also increase the suggestive effect by linking the question with a compliment: "As an experienced sales manager, you must agree with me that ..." or "Someone like you who knows this market, surely can't dispute the fact that ..."

2. Be very careful about using this method on prospective customers who are unsure of themselves or not very talkative. There is a great danger that they will agree with you out of politeness or convenience whilst they simultaneously think differently. Such an "*agreement obtained under lack of understanding*" will get you nowhere. The unspoken doubts are still there.

3. Don't form long chains of leading confirmation questions. The "Yes-frame" rhythm (once a person starts saying "yes" they are more likely to continue saying it), which you are trying to encourage the customer into, can hit-

the-buffers without warning. Then your prospect will feel manipulated and is likely to get nasty.

So you'll get one step nearer to a successful conclusion if your answers to Closed Information Questions made by the customer are linked with counter-questions which demand an answer.

Here is an example of linked questions during a sale

Prospective Customer: Do you carry out the installation yourselves?

Professional Seller: Yes we can. Should I make plans for us to do the assembly or would you prefer your people to do it?

Prospective Customer: Do you work with consignment stocks?

Professional Seller: Rarely. But if you want a consignment stock that will certainly be possible. May I just call my sales management to confirm?

Prospective Customer: What period do you usually allow for payment?

Professional Seller: Our standard terms are ten days 2% cash discount or thirty days net. How would you like to pay?

So if your customer decides to go ahead, then one detail of the order will have been settled and in most cases the order itself will have been silently agreed.

3

Stop selling: start asking "SWOT"

Quality QUESTIONS create a quality life.
Successful people ask better QUESTIONS,
and as a result, they get better answers.

ANTHONY ROBBINS: AMERICAN SELF HELP GURU

All courtroom lawyers know it. It is part of their basic training. They prepare very carefully beforehand to make sure they get it right. It is in the mythical law training book: "How to be a Lawyer – 101." It states that: *In a Court of Law you should never ask a question that you don't know the answer to.*

And the same goes for *all* successful sellers in every type of business.

Up to this point in the book you have seen that any question in the selling process is generally preferable to a statement. You have also read about the various rules and principles of questioning. Unless you understand these principles you will find it harder to take action when the customer doesn't react as expected.

It's just like a commercial pilot who must have a basic under-standing of manual flying skills and old-fashioned analogue instruments, before he is shown how to use the in-flight computer in the glass-cockpit (computer screen) of a mod-ern jet airliner. These days this computer can do most of the work for him including the landing, but he still must know how to do it manually if ever the computer doesn't work cor-rectly.

So it is with selling. What you are about to discover is the selling equivalent of the in-flight computer. I call it "**SWOT**". In this case **SWOT** is not the well-known management acronym for use in the analysis and examination of new projects: **S**trengths, **W**eaknesses, **O**pportunities and **T**hreats. For professional sellers it represents a set of really powerful sales questions.

First of all you can't start selling until you have got this cus-tomer (the one you are speaking to now) to "fess" up in areas in which you have an answer. You know what the answer should be, but will this ~~witness~~ *customer* give you the one you want?

So with this knowledge under your belt you can prepare to pace the "investigation phase" with the following classes of question:

Set-up Questions

Worry Questions

Overtone Questions

Turnaround Questions

And you actually endeavour to use them in this order during the investigation phase to gradually increase the desire of the prospect for a solution.

1. **Set-up questions**. These give you the "lie of the land", the foundation of the customer's business, how many people, what equipment, which places, type of customers, market position and so on. Much of this information these days can be discovered, quite simply, on the internet. However too many of these questions and your sale can go wrong very early. And most amateur sellers DO ask too many – Why? I ask this question at most of the sales master-classes I run and most experienced sales people give the answer immediately: "They are EASY." That's the only reason … they require no preparation.

   The thing that makes too-many-background-questions sales killers is that the customer feels interrogated; there is nothing in them for the questioned person. After a few too many of these the customer will get bored.

   "Where are your UK Offices?"

   "What will you do next?"

   "How many dealers do you have here?"

   "Why are you only operating in the USA?"

   "When are you considering making these changes?"

   However they can also confirm your understanding of a situation which is often a *very* useful thing to do. More than once I have put-my-foot-in-it by NOT asking confirming *background* questions: "Mr. Etherington is this machine heavy?" "Heavy? ... no ... not really heavy at all!" "Ah that's a pity we need a heavy one here. If it's too light the staff will move it around!" WHAT?

And ... "So tell me Mr. Etherington, is this system very easy to use?" "Easy? ... Mr. Prospect a child could use it!" "Oh well, we need something which is *not* so easy here. There needs to be a counter-intuitive step so that our people have to think before they set it in motion." OH NO!

In both these cases I should have confirmed my understanding of what they were asking me: "Is weight a particular issue for you?" "Is there any particular reason you are concerned about ease of use?"

As a question is generally always better than a statement, you can use background questions to tell the customer something without appearing to and thereby keep hold of his jacket at points "X" and "Y" (see page 34):

"Did you know that our company has just merged with Acme?" [We just merged with Acme.]

"Have you attended many of those typically useless corporate training programmes?" [Most corporate training is a waste of time.]

And also to find out if you are being "spun-a-line":

"Did you get your proposal from 'Track Ltd' at the Excel trade show?" [Track Ltd were not exhibiting at the trade show ... so their answer will tell you a lot.]

OK, so you now have some insight into the background to this client. So it is time to find out a bit more about some of the reasons he might be persuaded to buy your product with Worry Questions.

2. **Worry questions.** *Yes, questions about worries.* This might be the most important part of this chapter (let me read back a few pages). Yes it is ... so you might want to put an X at the top of this page with your pencil or pen ... or maybe turn the corner down ... anyway mark it.

To illustrate why this type of question is at the heart of really successful selling is best done by requesting that you indulge me for a minute. Will you do that? Thank you. Here goes:

I am about to ask you a question which has been a show-stopper here in my London apartment. On more than one occasion, when my business was just starting out, I used to ask this question of crumpled senior executives sitting round my dining room table (I didn't have an office then). They were usually seeking cut-price sales training and guessed (incorrectly) that I didn't (yet) have the clout to resist their discount demands. But this question alone often convinced them that I had some sort of insight into the reason their sales might not be succeeding very well so they paid my fee in full.

Here's the question:

What problem does your product or service solve?

I am always amazed that so many businesses are able to sell anything without having asked themselves this question. I am equally amazed that, if they've been reasonably successful so far, they haven't realized how much better their sales results would be if they did bother to ask it. So let me ask you (dear reader) again:

What problem does your product or service solve?

The reason it is an important "show stopping" question is that there is no other reason for your product or business to exist, other than its ability to solve a problem (or problems) for your customer. Your sales approach, the questions you ask, your website, your brochure, your product designers, your marketeers should all focus on that question(s) and the answer(s) you provide.

The inability of so many senior executives to answer this question about their own products is alarming. The crumpled gentlemen at my dining room used to look at each other, clear their throats and talk about technology or their company. Here is part of what one "e-business-man" told me when I asked what Internet problem his product solved for his customers:

"Well in the next few years everybody is going to bleed out in to multimedia and there'll be more competition. The various boxes that companies have grown up in, well, that's over. The impact of these mergers we all know about is that everybody will be multiplatform and multimedia, monetizing in each other's space and it's going to be an exciting world but it will be confusing. That's the message we're selling."

Yes, really. I'm sure there's a solution to *something* in all that waffle but, for the life of me, I can't see it.

But once you have identified what problems your product can typically fix for your customers then you are ready to start asking "Worry Questions".

Worry Questions are all about the problems which your product or service is designed to fix. They are gently probing in nature. They ask about the worries, problems, issues, costs and so on, that the problem (the one – *or several* – that your company's product can fix) is causing. Once you know which particular problems this customer (the one you are sitting across the table from) is most "worried" about, you know how to focus the rest of your sales meeting.

Anything else you can offer is superfluous so don't mention it again or you WILL get price objections (more on this later).

Worry Questions are such a built-in part of my corporate psyche, that when potential customers call my sales training business to enquire about the range of training we offer, ALL my staff are trained to ask, "Yes certainly … could you tell me about the sort of problem you need to address so that I know exactly what you're looking for?"

This kicks-off the sales process very quickly; *our ability to solve a problem is our only value from the customer's point of view.*

To focus more tightly on the exact issues which are most important (and worrying) for your customer, your Worry Questions, when face to face with the customer, might look like this:

"What is the main concern you have with respect to your central heating?"

"How much of a headache is this office design likely to become?"

"If this project does not go well will it cause any panic in the company?"

"What particular worries do you have with regard to your current sales team?"

"If this went wrong how would it affect your department?"

"Has office cleaning been a painful exercise to get 'right' here?"

Notice how each chatty "Worry Question" has an "unhappy" worry word in it: "concern", "headache", "panic", "worries", "wrong", "painful". This is because you wouldn't be sitting there "asking" if you didn't have a solution to a problem that caused a particular worry.

At this stage there is no way you could describe any of your questions as "jolly". Your customer doesn't want "jolly" and neither do you. The more your customer talks about those worries (in areas where you have a solution) the more their brain focuses on them. And the more their brain focuses the closer you are getting to your sale.

Once you have asked your Worry Questions (I will show you EXACTLY how to compose these for **your** company or product in the next chapter) you are in a strong position. You have information and understanding because you can now see the same iceberg which is causing your customer some measure of worry, headache or anxiety. You know its outline, colour, danger-factor, size and texture. Your customer can see it too because they've been describing it to you (with a bit of *prompting,* agreed). And they've been doing most of the talking so it's their own iceberg and not one you've been trying to *tell* them about with the usual hopeless sales pitch. So, job done ... time to tell them about your solution. Err ... well I wouldn't if I were you. Not yet anyway.

> This is not the end ... It is not the beginning of the end ... It is the end of the beginning.
>
> WINSTON CHURCHILL: UK PRIME MINISTER

The end of the beginning. Most amateur sellers DO see this as the end of the investigative process. They are bursting to tell the prospect all about their product or service ... they just can't wait! And out it all comes. The boiler-plate presentation – the sight-selling book with all the nice pictures – the ubiquitous laptop presentation.

I know it still happens like this because, for reasons beyond the scope of this book, a very senior executive from my local utility supplier has just been sitting at my dining room table trying to sell me a new natural gas central heating boiler ... OH DEAR! Why did he think that I would I want to see pictures of an "iron-trap" deep inside the works of it all? A picture of a radiator tap? Or a little film about what "condensate" looks like coming out of the outside vent? All because I just *might* be in the market for a new something to make hot water ... that's all.

You see, the thing is, the *only* thing your customer has confessed to you, is that they have a *bit of a problem now* or can see *a bit of a problem coming*. And, from the customer's perspective, that problem might well be containable at no significant extra cost. (Like my small boiler problem.) After all that's what managers and business owners are there for isn't it? To solve problems. If it wasn't for problems they wouldn't have a job would they, eh?!

So you can be pretty sure, even after your Worry Questions, the customer is saying in their head something like: "Yep OK I agree ... there IS a problem ... maybe a bit of a worry ... BUT is it really worth the likely cost and all the attendant hassle of the solution this guy's trying to sell me, to fix it?"

This is where you (the increasingly professional seller) move up a gear to *Overtone Questions*.

3. **Overtone questions.** Imagine driving your car into your local car service centre for its annual vehicle safety check. As you drive into the parking bay the owner greets you and waves at you to slow down pointing at your front, nearside tyre. "Anything wrong?" you ask. "Not particularly," replies the man "Its just that the tread on that tyre looks a bit worn."

You stop the engine and get out of the car to examine the tyre yourself. "Mmm," you agree. "I suppose it looks a bit worn. But there's still quite a bit of tread on it. Will it pass the test or not?" "Yes I think it'll just about pass the official test," he replies. "In that case I'll leave it till next time," you say and hand over the keys before departing.

Result: you leave the premises having convinced yourself that a "borderline pass" tyre is OK for you to drive on (well it *is* just inside the legal minimum) and the garage owner has missed a chance to sell you a new tyre (or two).

On the other hand ... how much more powerful would it have been if the service centre owner had said, "Yes I think it'll just about pass the official test. But did you see this article in the Car Expert magazine last month? It was about the recent tests carried out on borderline tyres, like this one, in wet weather. I have it here ... if you read this paragraph it says that even though it's 'legal', drivers are still 80% more likely to get into a skid on greasy road surfaces."

"Mmm, that's interesting," you say glancing at the article. As you read, your memory is prompted to recall the motoring programme on TV about police skid-pan training; would you remember to "turn into" the skid (whatever "turn into" means) if your car got a bit out of control on a slippery road?

The garage owner gets his little tyre tread depth-gauge and places it on your tyre. "You can see here the depth remaining on your tyre [he reads the gauge] is just over 6 mm and the minimum legal limit is 5 mm. How do you feel about that? ... a little over a millimeter!"

"A millimeter isn't much is it? How are the other tyres? We'd better have a look."

"I already have," says the centre owner. "The two on the rear are fine. The other front tyre is a bit better than its neighbour but it is advisable to change them both so that your steering doesn't get out of balance."

"Are two tyres expensive?"

"Well a single tyre, including fitting, will be £60 but if you buy two the total cost will be just £100. So which do you prefer?"

"Ah well … I guess I'd better take the two to be safe."

SOLD!

What the service centre owner was doing in the second example was applying what we call **Overtone Questions**. He was telling you the truth but by asking you questions. The questions were designed to get you to think about the knock-on effects of not addressing the apparently not-immediately-urgent issue of the rapidly wearing tyre.

It is rather like looking at an iceberg. Your first Worry Questions reveal the tip of the iceberg which might concern the potential customer. The subsequent Overtone Questions make the customer think about (and indeed *imagine*) the knock-on effects of not addressing the issue immediately.

Notice that there is very little "telling" involved in the persuasive process; the focus is on getting the customer to say the words you would otherwise have to *tell* her (or him). And, as such, has a much stronger psychological effect on the customer. Why is that? (I hear you ask.)

Two facts about persuasion. A huge amount of academic research has revealed something very interesting about humans when we are making decisions:

i We place a much greater persuasive value on the *words that come out of our own mouth* compared with those we hear from other people.

ii We place equally high persuasive value on the things we *ask for* compared with the things that we're offered but have NOT asked for.

The process of answering questions (however casually asked) has a strong, powerful and persuasive effect on every human brain. This is because the successful persuader is simply getting the customer to think about and "*verbalize*" genuine problems that might have to be faced if a solution to them is not found. And in getting the customer to both "think" and "talk", the seller is tapping into the most persuasive tool of all; the customer's imagination.

For, in all our heads, *our sub-conscious mind does not know the difference between real experiences and imagined experiences. And, as Einstein said: "When imagination and reality are in conflict the* imagination always wins".

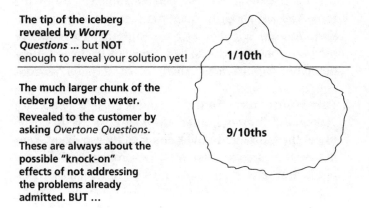

The tip of the iceberg revealed by *Worry Questions* ... but NOT enough to reveal your solution yet!

1/10th

The much larger chunk of the iceberg below the water.

Revealed to the customer by asking *Overtone Questions*.

These are always about the possible "knock-on" effects of not addressing the problems already admitted. BUT ...

9/10ths

still too early to reveal your solution! Read on ...

What do you mean ... still to early to sell? Yes it is; because you have one more phase to go before bringing out your solution. I know you are probably busting to do it immediately but as I pointed out back on page 42 all the available research into sales psychology indicates that the longer you can stay in the "investigation" phase the better the outcome will be for you.

So, yes your questions have helped to focus the prospective customer's attention on areas in which you have a solution and where the customer has a problem (or two). But you're still in "*SELLER-to-buyer*", mode, where up to now you have been controlling things. It is time now to make the customer feel even more in control before you demonstrate your solution. You're about to get jolly, happy, smiley, over the moon!

Up until now the best that can be said of your questions (chatty and conversational though they have been) is that they varied from the "bland" to the "unhappy" to the "how bad could it get". So, you are about to change the tone. You are about to obey the second fact of persuasion. You are about to get the customer to request a solution. You are about to be introduced to the last question type: *Turnaround Questions.*

4. **Turnaround questions.** "Happy Face" is the symbol for *Turnaround Questions*. Until now your objective has been to get the customer to think about all the troubling, worrisome things connected with the problem which your product or service can fix. You have been steadily "building the pain" from the bland "Set-up Questions" through

"Worry Questions" and on to "Overtone Questions". Represented "facially" the value-creation process would look like this:

Set-up....................Worry................Overtone............Turnaround

Now having shown them the way down into the "Vale of Despair" it is time to show them the Light! Or at least let them see the possible way out.

When you use *Turnaround Questions* you are, for the first time, encouraging the customer to talk his way out of the hole. It is the first time in the meeting that the tone of your questions encourages the customer to think how much better things could be. All the other questions have been about problems and worries, now you can allow your prospect to think about the happy result of taking your solution.

"Mr. Prospect I now have a better idea of how your business operates and some of the issues you face. Can you tell me briefly how a solution to the two main problems you have described, "speed" and "accuracy", would help you here?"

"Mrs. Prospect these constant breakdowns with your central heating boiler are obviously getting quite problematic and expensive for you. So if there was a perfect solution to the problems you've described, what would it look like?"

"So in a perfect world, at the end of the first three months of a successful sales training programme, what would be happening in your sales force that's not happening now?"

"OK ... thank you for detailing the current issues. So based on those facts ... what are your criteria for a replacement IT system and ... how will you measure the criteria?"

Do you notice in all the *Turnaround Questions* the investigation is no longer into the surface worries or the overtones inherent in not addressing them? Instead the "professional" seller asks (encourages) the customer to state how a solution to these issues (if one exists) will change things for the better. The seller has been asking questions up to now which focus on areas where he has a solution so this is where the customer's focus is too.

It all goes back to Socrates. Is this all theory? Do customers really want to be kept in a state of anticipative suspense? Is it really effective in practice? "Yes", "Maybe" and "It is".

If you have ever watched a clown about to "custard-pie" a fellow clown for the benefit of a children's audience, you will notice that the "pie-in-the-face" punch line is not where the joke lies. For the kids it is all in the interactive anticipation. The clown will parade in front of the kids for up to a minute looking for support to "pie" his unsuspecting slapstick colleague, "So kids, shall I ... [kids shout encouragement] shall I? ... [kids go mad and stand on their seats] shall I?" [Kids go berserk, "Do it! ... dooo it!"] The actual custard pie moment is almost an anti-climax.

Have you ever watched the TV ad-fo-mercials on satellite and cable TV channels for products such as "Wonder vegetable peelers" and "Miracle carpet sweepers"? If you are ever up in the early hours of the morning you may well have seen them. They are massively profitable. Next time you're up in the early hours look at these selling machines critically. You will notice one thing; they keep from telling you the price for as long as possible. They talk about all the problems you face without their product. They show the mess your kitchen gets into (or could get into ... if it hasn't yet it soon will). They pour soot, powder, flour and mud on to carpets and grind it in, then get the TV audience to agree what a nightmare it is (if it hasn't happened yet it soon will). They eventually show the product in action ... miracle! ... But how much is it? How much? [Not yet ... not yet ... we want to show you more nightmares] Only when they have you fully softened up with nightmares do they finally tell you ... "Just three payments of $29.99! Order now to avoid disappointment. Call the number on your screen ... NOW!"

The people who operate country and state lotteries all over the world have analysed the behaviour of people who buy Lottery tickets. They have found that lottery-ticket-buyers are at their peak in terms of "happiness" at the moment of selecting their numbers and buying their tickets. The moment of peak anticipation, when the "draw" is still several hours or days away is the best moment of all. As the draw gets closer the happiness and confidence gradually decreases. The moment of least optimism is when the numbers are being called.

There is a famous story about the philosopher Socrates who was approached one day in the market by a young man.

"Master," he asked. "When will you take me on as a student?"

Socrates said nothing but led the lad down to the river, took him into the water and pushed his head beneath the surface and put his foot on it. After another 15 seconds or so, the boy started to struggle, but still Socrates kept his foot hard down. After 30 seconds the lad was starting to panic and squirm but still the foot remained in place. After a further 15 seconds the lad was thrashing madly and clearly needed to take an urgent life-saving breath. After a few more seconds the wily Socrates reached down and yanked the boy's head above the surface of the water and allowed him to take his first breath in nearly one minute.

As he recovered the gasping spluttering boy naturally asked Socrates a question which was right at the front of his mind, "What did you do that for!?"

"Because," replied Socrates. "I will not take you on as a student until your need for knowledge is as great as your need for air was a couple of minutes ago!"

And that's the way it is with effective selling.

If you want to sell your product for "top dollar" you must first have your prospective customer in a state of deep desire for your solution. The longer you can keep them starved of a solution, yet still talking and thinking about the problem, the greater their "wants" and "needs" become. The greater the "need" or "want", then the greater the value created in your customer's own head.

When you're "selling" you are getting the customer, who was probably having the average *person's* "Sort-of-OK-day" until you arrived, to think about "problems" they'd rather not think about. Or to think about problems they have simply not bothered to think about until now. So your chatty questions make them think about their problems ... they can't help it.

Questions always take full control of our brain's conscious focusing power. By first getting this thinking process going you will trigger (eventually) a desire for a solution.

If we represent the average person's day by the little graph below in which **"+10"**, represents a really great day and **"−10"** represents a state of *anxious despair* day, then the sales "self-persuasion" process becomes a little clearer.

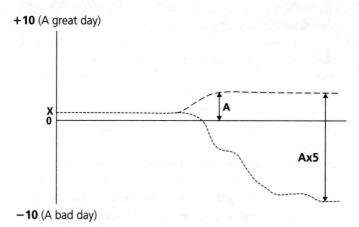

+10 (A great day)

X
0

A

Ax5

−10 (A bad day)

As you can see your average person ("X") – in this case a potential customer – is having a slightly above average "OK day" ... a bit above the norm ... nothing much to complain about really i.e. a bit better than the "0" line on my little chart.

First an average "Amateur Seller" approaches the prospective customer and after a few cursory questions, makes his pitch or presentation. The customer finds this mildly interesting and perceives there is some *possible* value in the proposition. This raises their view of the day by a few notches (value, in the customer's mind, in this mediocre sales meeting, is represented by the letter "A"). At the end of the meeting they ask the seller for a brochure and say that they will "let him know". And they may do that ... when they get round to it ... soon probably ... maybe. The Amateur Seller thinks he's done all he can do. It is all in the lap of the gods. He is wrong.

The trained professional seller, approaching the same potential customer, asks "Worry Questions" followed by "Overtone Questions". These have the reverse effect. They make the customer think about problems and the knock-on effects of problems (the ones his product can solve).

The customer just can't help thinking about the problems because they're answering questions and talking about them. And their "OK day", at a deeply subconscious level, begins to move below the "not a good day, not a bad day" line to a "–5".... or well below that.

HOWEVER when the seller finally takes his foot off the prospect's head, which he does, either today or several meetings later, the value of the solution (the oxygen equivalent) is represented in the graph as "Ax5" or more. In other words, *much* greater perceived value in the customer's head.

So as far as a customer is concerned ...

the only value the manufacturer of chairs has ...
the only value a bank has ...
the only value a supermarket has ...
the only value a car manufacturer has ...
the only value a builder has ...
the only value a software company has ...
the only value a hotel has ...
the only value a publisher has ...
the only value a clothing manufacturer has ...
the only value a dentist has ...
the only value a TV company has ...
the only value a newspaper has ...
the only value a website has ...
the only value a printer has ...
the only value YOUR product or service has ...
is its ability to solve a problem.

So, to sell your product, you need to get your prospective customer thinking about problems (a lot) before you start to show them your solution.

Final points

Your customer will do quite well with or without your product.

Yes, they will have a perfectly acceptable life ... whatever!

So you need to get real if you're not going to get beaten.

4

Features, advantages and benefits

A prudent question is one-half of wisdom.

FRANCIS BACON: PHILOSOPHER AND
LORD CHANCELLOR OF ENGLAND (1521–1626)

"It's all very unfair. They should be interested in everything about us. Well I don't care … we've worked our socks off to build this business and they're damn well going to hear about it!"

To repeat a point already made in this book most of your customers couldn't care less about your products or services. They only want to know what they can DO for them. They want to know how they will solve some problem, remove a worry, or help them achieve some business or career objective. Too often, amateur sellers concentrate on the great features of their company or product. They talk about how long they've been in business (*who cares?*), how delighted they are to announce the opening of their new office (*so what?*), that they offer 24 hour service (*so do hundreds of competitors*) their regular newsletters (*boring*) or that they attend all the trade shows (*yeah right!*). But every time they neglect to translate these "features" into the real motives for buying.

In order to ask questions that will get your customer to persuade themselves, you now need to have a bit of a "think" about what it is you are selling. And once again I will help you. Any old question won't do. Your questions must be about aspects of your product or service. In order to compose your persuasive questions you must have a detailed understanding about three aspects of every product or service on the face of the earth. I call them Features Advantages and Benefits.

What's a feature?

A feature is an objective, a raw fact and observable characteristic of your product or service. Features don't change whether the prospect buys it or not. For example, some features of your planned trade show might include room for 200 booths, five break-out rooms, and 3500 visitors over three days.

Features of a newsletter you publish might include 32 pages, a colour cover, and a bingo reply card. A feature of your building company might be a guaranteed cost estimate on any quotation.

Features are statements you make like: "24 hour service" "Nationwide coverage" "We are a training company" We are experts in this field" "Our service is tailored to your requirements".

What's an advantage?

An advantage is what the feature does, the service that it performs for your potential customer. To turn any feature into an advantage imagine you have just mentioned it to your customer and they have asked, quite curtly: "So what?!" An advantage is your answer to that question. For example, an advantage of having break-out rooms at your trade show is that they attract qualified attendees to your exhibits. The advantage of something like a bingo reply card is that it makes it easier for your customers to respond.

The areas in which most customers are seeking solutions are called the "Four Ps" (**P**ower, **P**rofit, **P**restige and **P**leasure) so it is wise to ensure that your answer to the "So what?" directly or by implication, addresses at least one of these.

The Four Ps

Power

Anything to do with *control* over events, people, money, markets or things. Early adopters of new ideas are often doing it to gain an edge over their rivals. Many very wealthy people are not turned-on by money because they have all they could ever need. The money they can generate from buying your product or adopting your idea is secondary to the *Power* they might gain over their rivals. For many rich and powerful people it is not enough to win against a rival it is also necessary to call the rival after the event and remind them that they have just lost. Power is a big turn on for many successful people.

Profit

Making money or cutting costs is what the *profit* motive is all about. If the particular feature you're considering could address a problem in a money area then write it down. I am often told that it is always about money when you're selling everything but it really isn't. Also bear in mind that one feature could solve a problem for more than one of the "Four Ps", so write them all down.

Prestige

Why do some people drive a "Mini" and others drive a "Rolls Royce"? Why do some people fly "First Class" and others go "Economy"? Why do my own children refuse to shop in one particular supermarket chain and always chose a more expensive one? In all cases the end result is the same. The car drivers still get from their chosen A to B. The air passengers get to the same holiday destination at the same time whether in the front or the back of the airplane. The food brands sold in both supermarket chains are the same. So what's going on? It is the *prestige* motive. Is there anything inherent in a feature of your product that could address a possible prestige or self-esteem problem? Write it down.

Pleasure

This is probably the most basic driver of all. It includes ease-of-use, simplicity, availability, touch, feel, sensation, odour, sex, beauty, artistic quality and soothing sounds. And in addition it covers looks, colour, attractiveness and taste. If your product's features address any potential problem in the *pleasure* area, then note it next to the appropriate feature.

Knowing your product's *advantages* is extremely important. What your product "does" to solve a potential problem is the only value it has for your customer. Your advantages are the things that should be mentioned in your brochures and all your other advertising banners and materials. Most promotional material generated by most companies is packed with features. I don't get it ... and neither will their customers.

What's a benefit?

But that's not the whole story. Advantages are potential *benefits*. And *benefits* are the most important things you offer for all your customers. A benefit is the pay-off provided by the advantage, or the value it provides to this individual prospect, to solve an explicit problem. A benefit is a solution.

Think of all benefits as the value of the advantage to the individual prospect. These are therefore defined by your prospects' goals and problems.

The same product or service you are selling, may offer different benefits to prospects with different problems to solve. If your company is in business to organize trade shows and business conventions your feature might mean different things to different people. For the trade show go-getters, a busy floor with lots of traffic may be just the opportunity they've been waiting for to introduce a new machine.

Another client might want to participate in order to network with the show's other exhibitors. Yet a third may view it as an opportunity to orient their new employees to their industry. The professional seller always links features and advantages to their prospects' objectives, so they can clearly see the benefits. They do this by compiling and preparing questions in advance that focus on areas in which they potentially have solutions.

Also remember that a benefit may not be intuitively obvious. Professional sales people target their selling message by always translating features into advantages into benefits. For example, you might say, "One *feature* of our training seminar is that delegates will have paid \$99.00 each to enter the exhibit hall and attend the whole exhibition. The *advantage* is that these are customers who really want to see what you have to offer in this particular market, and you *benefit* because that makes it easier for you to sell to them."

Because the same features will offer different benefits to different prospects, the professional salesperson will target their presentation to cover only selected features that offer a clear advantage to a particular customer: "Attendees will have paid $99.00 to enter the exhibit hall. The *advantage* is that by keeping the traffic down to a manageable level, your people *benefit* by having time to qualify each visitor, rather than just passing out literature to a crowd."

Before setting out to sell anything new, carry out this simple exercise. Take a sheet of A4 paper and place it lengthways in front of you. Draw two lines from top to bottom dividing the sheet into three equal sections. Head the first column with the title "Features" and list the ten major features of your product or service. Head the second column "Advantages" and list several advantages for each feature. And in the third column, list the possible "Benefits" of each Advantage for the different types of prospects you plan to call on. It doesn't matter what you're selling, your presentations will flow naturally and logically across the page, making it easier for prospects to justify buying.

That's one way ... do you want to know how to make it even more powerful?

Let the customer identify the benefits for themselves. You know the Advantages but your Worry Questions (Chapter 3) will actually get them thinking about explicit problems.

This always makes me think of the US TV game show *Jeopardy* in which the contestant is given the answer: "the

Pentagon" and has to think, "If that's the answer then what was the possible question? ... What is the headquarters of the United States Department of Defense?"

For a professional sales person the *advantages* are your "answers". So you use these advantages as a basis for forming the specific "Worry Questions". For example, the answer is: "We provide a 24 hour security service so you don't have to concern yourself with night time burglaries". So your Worry Question might be: "Have you been concerned by the number of break-ins in this part of town in the past six months?"

So to recap, a *feature* is what your company, product or service is or does (this car has ultrasonic parking sensors fitted to each bumper and electronic power-steering). A *benefit* is what it will do for your customer (it will help you park in small spaces without risking damaging your car).

It has been an unbreakable rule of successful selling since the early 20th century, that your *features* don't sell, but the *benefits* (solutions), inherent in those features, do. And to elevate yourself from amateur seller to professional you must apply this to all your sales presentations, and all your conversations with customers. Also to your marketing literature, brochures, flyers, letters and advertisements. The more you illustrate how your business or specific product will help solve your prospective customer's problems or "wants", the more you demonstrate *benefits*, the more successful your sales efforts will be.

It is true that some of your customers may want to know about some of your features, so that they can ascertain what's included in your price, but it's the *benefits* your product offers that will actually sell your product or service.

You must develop every one of your product features into a tangible benefit, an end-result that satisfies a customer problem or "want".

So what? What's in it for me? (The Advantage "black hole".) I'd like you always to remember to place yourself in your customer's shoes and ask "What's In It For Me?" **So what?** … if the laptop you're trying to sell me has a 867MHz processor, 256MB memory, a 20 inch display and built in Bluetooth? **What problem will that solve for me?!**

And don't fall into the common black hole of simply developing your *features* into *advantages* – how a product or service COULD POSSIBLY be used or COULD POSSIBLY help a prospective customer, or how it compares with your competitor's product. It is a lazy way of selling … it marks you down as an "amateur". What does it mean for this customer? The one you are with right now. What will they be able to do as a result? Ask them to tell you.

True *benefits* are only really *benefits* if they deal directly with a customer "want" explicitly stated by the customer. For example, consider a new lawn mower with the feature: "Power driven Qualfast 20 horse-power engine". "It's the fastest grass cutter on the market" isn't a benefit – it is an *advantage*. The *benefit* is that you can mow your lawn in half the normal time, which allows you more time to enjoy your garden. The true benefit to the customer is revealed if the customer has already stated, "Yes I really want to find a way to cut the time I spend walking up and down behind my mower".

Many small businesses are set up specifically to address a need, solve a particular problem or fill a market niche. Your *raison d'e-tre* is to offer a clear benefit to your prospective customers.

So don't fall into the black hole of getting over-enthusiastic about all your "stuff": your length of time in business, your history, your product's gizmos and baroque knobs and whirls, and its new, unique and revolutionary features.

Don't focus on the bells and whistles. All your buyer cares about is one thing – what will it DO for me?

You must think *FAB* – Features, Advantages, Benefits. Always be seeking *true* benefits. The secret of coming up with these genuine benefits is to be truly customer-oriented. Ask "Worry Questions" to reveal the key areas of concern to the customer. Then ask "Overtone Questions" (it's all in this book) to make them want your solution as much as a living creature needs air. The benefit you give is much more powerful if it fits a specific, explicit customer "want" stated by your customer.

If you are a senior executive in your organization ask someone to bring you all your sales and marketing material. Do it now. You can't afford to wait; selling is your most important company activity. Look through it all and rethink your "boiler-plate" sales pitches. Is it all "Established since 1950" stuff? Is there a lot of third party text: "Customers will admire our new higher speed service"? Did you write it? Oh dear … chuck it out quietly … it isn't selling. Now, how can you turn your features and advantages into benefits?

If you think all this is theoretical codswallop, most professional, successful sales-oriented organizations don't. And at the same time many large organizations could do a lot better. Last Sunday I tore out some weekend newspaper and colour-magazine ads (see below). I want you to see how the text in advertisements 3 and 4 offers potential customers tangible benefits, whilst 1 and 2 just presents features and advantages.

1. **Magazine advertisement for mobile phone company O2.** Video Media Messaging/Games/Downloads/Music/Sport/Entertainment [ALL FEATURES] Get into O2 Active.

2. **Newspaper advertisement for Philips Philishave Shaver.** Each of the three rotary-action shaving heads has 90 omni-directional slots [FEATURE] to catch all the hairs, irrespective of length and angle to the skin [ADVANTAGE]. The shaving heads also float independently to ensure they follow every contour of your face [ADVANTAGE]. The double action cutters [FEATURE] lift each hair to achieve a closer shave [ADVANTAGE] and there is also a pop-out trimmer for sideburns [FEATURE].

3. **Magazine advertisement for Mercedes-Benz.** SBC is the world's first brake-by-wire system [FEATURE]. When it's raining, SBC even helps keep the brake discs dry by clearing water from the surface of the disc [FEATURE]. All measures which combine to reduce your stopping distance by more than 3% [ADVANTAGE]. SBC: only a split second quicker than normal braking. But then accidents can happen in a split second [BENEFIT].

4. **Magazine advertisement for Lady Protector**. The Lady Protector is the only women's razor with wire wrapped blades [FEATURE] to protect you from nicks and cuts [ADVANTAGE]. So it doesn't matter how speedily you whiz down a leg or zoom around an ankle [BENEFIT]. It always leaves you racetrack smooth. [BENEFIT].

My hero in the world of professional selling is Neil Rackham, author of the book *SPIN Selling*. He is an academic who applied some serious research into what works and what doesn't when sales people are trying to sell things to other people. His research has shown that the higher the value of the sale, the less effective Advantages become, and the more effective Benefits become. So you can see that the more you relate your message to an explicit customer problem (e.g. You can avoid accidents, shave as quickly as you want without "nicks") the better.

And how can you find out what your customer's "wants", "headaches" and "problems" are? You ask questions: investigate the knock-on effects, consequences and implications of your customer's explicit problems. What benefits and solutions are they seeking? You do what business owners large and small are very good at – get close to your customers.

True benefits

The deeper and more explicit the benefit you can use to appeal to your customer, the more powerful your sales argument.

When my local health club in Marylebone, London advertised all the new American equipment they had installed, from running machines to weight-stacks and free weights, that was a list of their features.

When they revisited their selling strategy a few weeks ago and set up a promotional stand in my local subway station they did something different. They told the passing audience how "attendance for just 12 days under their special regime" would: "Give you the best body shape you ever had", that was a translation from feature to benefit.

But when I enquired at the stand they showed me pictures of men my age with sharply chiselled features, six-packs, and hardly-an-ounce-of-fat and all in less than two weeks ... Hey! ... They were working on *true* benefits! ... I bought the fitness programme ... and I knew what they were doing!

The more deeper, "explicit" benefits you can get the customer to think about and talk about, the much greater chance you are giving yourself of a successful sale. On the other hand the more you talk about your *features* the more your customer will think only about the **cost**.

Summary

You need to spend some time establishing the Features, Advantages and Benefits of your own product or service.

Once you have done this, for each Advantage and Benefit, write down one or more Worry Questions. *At the very least* you must try to ask your full set of Worry Questions before you either tell or show your prospective customer any of your product's benefits. Even then YOU MUST ONLY SHOW THE BENEFITS THAT THE CUSTOMER HAS SHOWN AN INTEREST IN FIXING. If you add in a whole bunch more then you *will* generate price objections.

Finally define the likely knock-on effects of NOT fixing the problem revealed by your Worry Questions. You will need these if the customer doesn't believe that it is worth the cost or hassle of addressing any of the issues revealed by your Worry Questions.

5

I object! (Objection overruled!)

Don't think much of the view!?
What did you expect to see out of a Torquay hotel
bedroom window!? Sydney Opera House perhaps? The
Hanging Gardens of Babylon? Herds of wildebeest
sweeping majestically across the plain!?

BASIL FAWLTY: HOTEL PROPRIETOR
BBC TV COMEDY *FAWLTY TOWERS* (1979)

Sales objections are GOOD things?

When I was a young trainee and a very Amateur Salesman in the early 1970s, Rank Xerox taught me that sales objections were good things. They taught us, in the old Xerox training school in Great Portland Street, London, that sales objections were actually buying signals in disguise. The more you heard during the sales process then the closer you were getting to a sale.

Alas ... it isn't true. Sorry.

An Amateur Seller's most natural reaction to being confronted by or presented with an objection is to get all defensive. "Defend and Attack" behaviour is a classic sign of an Amateur Seller in action. "You say it's too expensive? Well actually it isn't if you compare it with the other ways of achieving the same result and our company has worked hard to make sure we're competitive." Now we're diving into an argument. Great fun to watch ... a terrible way to persuade.

But now I have bad news and good news for you.

The bad news is that academic research in the mid 1970s into the way customers are persuaded to buy, shows that the MORE objections you hear the LESS likely you are to get the sale.

The good news is that selling-by-using-chatty-questions of the sort I have already described, will actually result in you hearing fewer objections. (HURRAH!) The reason for this is that you are finding out, in advance, what *is* and what *is not* of interest to your potential customer, *before* you show them your solution. The eventual presentation of your solution when you are ready will then be focused on those areas of interest ONLY and not peppered with lots of things of no interest to them and about which they would otherwise raise objections.

So that's all lovely isn't it? No more objections to deal with! ... err ... no ... not quite true – Sorry (again).

Selling is both a science (asking questions) and an art (in the eye of the beholder) so the other person's perception of the situation might not match yours exactly. How ever well you sell, you will get *some* objections that you have to deal with. And I am going to show you how.

Amateur seller cowardice ... begone!

The one thing I need you to avoid at the start is your collapsing into "instant cowardice" mode. "The instant cowardice mode?" you ask. "Whatever is that?"

On being confronted by a prospective customer who is raising all sorts of queries on your sales proposal, most non-sales executives (tough, rough, no-nonsense successful executives just like you) offer to cut the price; to offer a discount!

Listen! Are you listening? It is generally NOT about the price. Price is usually around number "5" or "6" on a list of 10 things important to your customer. Your customer (like you when you're a customer) wants *value for money* and will pay your price if you create enough value in their mind with the help of your questions.

I could make a lot of money by writing a book entitled: *The Comprehensive Book Of Answers To Every Sales Objection You Are Ever Likely to Hear*. The book would sell and sell. The point is that it would be totally worthless because every objection in sales has to be handled "in context". So, instead of listing a series of typical objections it will be more useful for you if I give you some tools to handle four classes of typical objections.

I will call them: "We do" "We don't" "How much?" and "Excuses".

Dealing with the classic sales objections

1. We do. Often you will find that, although your questioning has been exemplary and you believe that you have a complete picture of your customer's "worries" and "wants", actually your customer wasn't listening properly all the time. When you endeavour to finalize the sale an objection is raised, "But we really need a supplier who can deliver bathroom AND occasionally kitchen equipment. Your service is all bathroom oriented. We really need a more all-encompassing supplier."

As CEO of the county's fastest expanding complete bathroom and kitchen supplier you want to shout, "Weren't you listening a couple of meetings ago? I asked you about kitchen services and you said you weren't interested. Now you've changed your mind. I wish you'd make up your mind!"

What you, an amateur seller, actually says is, something like, "Oh yes, I'm sorry, we DO also supply kitchen equipment. I should have made that clearer before." But now you are moving into the realm of the Professional Seller you are going to do something a bit different and much more powerful. You are going to ask a question about something "we do":

"Yes, could you tell me a bit about your concerns with regard to this issue?"

"Well, we are finding that some of our satisfied customers, once we've installed their bathroom, ask us about doing their kitchen as well … and we don't want to let them down."

"So if we couldn't supply kitchen equipment too, that would present a growing problem?"

"Yes … increasingly. This is especially important to our Middle Eastern client base … we did ten major jobs in Dubai last year."

"I see so it is really important for you to be able to expand in this area?"

"Oh yes … we see the market growing by about 20% next year and we're projecting 25% the year after. It's is becoming VERY important."

See what's happening? You're getting your customer to think and talk about the issue of the apparent shortcoming in your proposal in an area in which you CAN help. He just doesn't know that yet. You have just asked a Turnaround Question and now, after your powerful build-up, you're going to finally reveal your solution.

"Mr. Prospect, as kitchens are clearly becoming at least as important as bathrooms to you now, you will be pleased to hear that we also offer a complete kitchen service too, supported by all the major manufacturers. So when you work with us we will be able to satisfy all your needs in this area too."

So, when a customer queries your abilities in an area in which "you do" have a solution then STOP and ask questions *before* you reveal your solution.

2. **We don't**. There are no perfect products. There are no perfect services. There are holes, all over the place, in your offering too. There is no magic wand you can wave to make it all come right. When a prospective customer tells the "average amateur" that their product is deficient in some way, the first reaction is often to rush back to base and attempt to modify, redevelop or change the design of their offering to accommodate. This often takes time effort and money. Also, by the time the seller gets back to the customer with the changes, things have moved on. The

requirement is not so pressing and another supplier has been found anyway. Your best way to handle an objection in an area in which your product or service *is* deficient is to "AIM": **A**cknowledge **I**solate **M**inimize.

You never tell a lie.

First you **Acknowledge** the customer's concern.

Then you **Isolate** the customer's objection.

Then you **Minimize** the effect by reminding them of all the things they have already told you they do like about your product in its current form. The benefits usually out-weigh the odd deficiency.

"Mr. Prospect, I fully understand why our lack of a perma-nent office in Singapore is an issue for you [Acknowledge] … is this the only thing that is of any concern now?" [Isolate]

"Yes … just for my own understanding could we just sum-marize all the benefits that you have said the 'Warmo Boiler' *will* provide to your installations. [Minimize] You said that the most important thing you liked was the reli-ability record of the 'Warmo' and that you had checked with other customers and were more than satisfied in this area. You also said that the free insurance was a major benefit because of the six-figure charge you have been paying elsewhere. And also the built in electric trolley for ease of re-location would avoid the delays you normally experience. Whilst I agree it would be additionally bene-ficial to have a permanent local office in Singapore our local agents will provide the level of service you need as testified by our 20 other local customers."

"Now ... the only thing remaining that we need to agree at this point is ..."

Note: you can link this last example to the Winston Churchill Balance Sheet technique shown on page 152.

3. **How much?** Fact: price is always an objection. It doesn't matter whether your product costs a little or a lot, somebody will always tell you that it is "far too much". That's just the way it is. If they jump too quickly, with a smile on their face – "YES!" – then your price is probably too low.

   The way to handle price objections with a "Driver" personality (rough, tough, successful, serial street-fighter types) is outlined on page 146. This is a rather special case as "Drivers" probably make up only 10% of all the buyers you will meet. The other 90% of customers are not in business just "for fun" and to "keep score" (as most Drivers are) so they are quite amenable to confident presentations of value.

   The choice of handling techniques you have for price objections is quite varied and can be used with most prospects. They are: "Yes" "Shock" "Cheap?" "Comparison" and "Slice".

Handling techniques

"Yes"
[Confidently smile] "Yes this product IS expensive. Let me show you why ..." Now summarize all the Benefits and Advantages the customer told you were important to him. DO NOT ADD ANYTHING ELSE OTHERWISE YOU WILL BE ASKED TO CUT THOSE EXTRAS OUT AND GIVE A DISCOUNT. Once you have done this you can go straight into a

Close: "So the only thing we really need to discuss now is whether the LCD or the Plasma is going to be best for you … what do you think?"

"Shock!"
"Shock" is a great tactic – probably my own favourite.

"Mr. Etherington your fees for this conference seem very high. You are very expensive!" [You must practice this and – oh yes, don't laugh – look genuinely surprised.] "Expensive?! Mr. Prospect I am very shocked that you should say that. Nobody has ever told me our fees are too high before. Would you mind telling me why you think that?"

You are forcing the customer to justify his objection. He will usually say: "Yes… we looked at several of your competitors, like 'Other Consultancy' and 'Tom and Dick Agency' and your fees are about 20% higher than the average." "Yes those are all very good companies. And of course with our company, in addition to the basic services they provide, you have also asked us for … [now present all the true benefits and advantages he previously discussed and revealed in the investigation phase] So looking at the total package does the fee seem reasonable?"

If your prospect still "makes-a-face" at your price, you have a choice between "Cheap" and "Compare". You can add technique three: "Cheap".

"Cheap"
"Cheap" is a direct challenge to your prospect's reason for buying the service. Keeping a straight face you say, "I'm sorry Mr. Prospect we are definitely not a cheap supplier but we are the best. I really didn't appreciate that price was your main issue. I can give you a list of several companies in this market who are cheaper

than us at the top end. Would you like it?" Most people hate that anyone should think them "cheap".

As I have to do this quite often I can tell you that my customers usually say, "Oh … ha ha … come on! Ha ha … we're not a 'cheap' company it's just that we have a budget for this sort of thing. Let's have a look again at what we need."

They then review – with my help and prompting – all the things they told me were very important benefits for them. More often than not we agree the deal at my original price with only a little good-natured grumbling. Occasionally they still grumble and *don't* agree to go ahead. In that case I generally say to them, "OK you win … could you tell me please what do you think a service like ours should cost?"

The last time I used this one was for a customer who complained about a customized training event I had organized in Prague. It was a great success but when he received the invoice with all the requested "extras" added in the final total was quite "lumpy". He just hadn't been keeping a check on his spending. He called me and told me this was double the figure he'd been expecting. I could have played hard-ball – we had A CONTRACT – but I really placed more value on our long-term relationship than this one assignment.

"OK James," I said. "Could you tell me what you think it was worth?" "Oh now you're placing me in a difficult position, Bob! That's not fair." "Well, what *was* it worth to you?"

He thought for a moment … and then quoted a price which was 90% of our invoice. "That's a deal James," I said. "Provided that you contract with us for another 30 days training assignments in the next 12 months." It was done.

And ... how shall I put it? Over the following 12 months we easily got back our minimum day-fee, averaged over all the projects (including Prague) and he had been able to save face into the bargain. Result!

Another way to handle the "price" objection is to "Compare".

"Compare"

If your customer is still "having a go" about your price, a quick technique is to say to them: "Too expensive? ... I'm surprised but ... could you tell me what you're comparing us with?" The prospect is then forced to illustrate using the names of several other companies in your field ... or waffle. "Yes ... well ... we've spoken to quite a few companies and they're all less than your price." "Could you tell me which companies in particular?" "Errr ... yes ... FigTree Ltd, we called them ... and um Rosebush and Co."

You should know your competitors well enough – well this IS your market – to know how to respond. If they are a lower end competitor you can say, "That's very interesting so are you saying that FigTree are offering the fully flexible contract, no cancellation fee and the completely bespoke product you are looking for and all for less price than ours?" Knowing FigTree as you do there is no way they can offer all this for a fraction of your price. The prospective customer is now going to have to lie, bluff or tell you they are "sure that is the case". Actually as soon as you've left the office they are going to re-check the information they have.

Sit tight. In 80% of these cases you'll end up with the business.

If, on the other hand, the competitor name(s) they give are at the top "Rolls Royce" end of the market (above where you're positioned), you can bet, pretty confidently, that their prices are going to be higher than yours.

NEVER, NEVER CRITICIZE YOUR COMPETITORS TO A CUSTOMER.

In this case say: "Yes, RoseBush are a *really* good company ... top of the market. And they are cheaper than us? Is that across the board or are they insisting on sticking to their standard non-customized package as usual?" "Err ... we have asked them to customize it." "And they're doing that for no charge? [you know they ALWAYS charge for customizing] You've got a good deal from them and they're probably not adding in their usual full fee for travel days [you know they ALWAYS 'whack' the client for full consultancy charges on travel days] is that right?" "I'll have to check ... are you saying all this is included in your fee?" They're yours!

Tell no lies ... just ask more questions in areas you know your competitors may be weak and YOU are strong! And finally there's "Slice".

"Slice"
"Slice" is more for service providers. When a service is to be provided on an annual basis but paid for "up-front" the bill can often appear alarming.

For many years I sold real-time financial information services for the global news agency Reuters. The end users were mainly young bank traders dealing in multimillion dollar currency exchanges every few minutes. Our services weren't cheap ... in fact they were very expensive! When decision makers baulked at £1000 per month per terminal per dealer, it didn't take buyers long to calculate that was £12,000 per annum per dealer and in each room there were 100 dealers! That was £1,200,000 per annum (and this was the 1980s, a quarter century ago from when I'm writing this).

When they baulked (and baulk they did) I discovered the easiest way to handle the objection was to slice it into bits and say, "Well, it seems a lot I agree. However if you take the average 20 working days in a month that works out at just £50 per day. That's £25 for the morning and just £12.50 up to mid-morning tea break. I'm sure each of your dealers are expected to earn more than £12.50 for your bank between 8.45 and 10.00am … aren't they?" Most traders in those heady days of the 80s were expected to earn 1000s of pounds in a morning's trading. So the mathematics was pretty obvious. The usual result was a rueful smile and a signature on the contract.

I still get this reaction when I sell my training services. And more often than not find prospective clients saying: "One trainer … £3000 for ONE day?! Why that's … that's … £15,000 for just one week!" When you ask the customer how much money each of the ten sales people is targeted to earn over the coming year as a result of our training programme it is usually several tens of thousands of pounds. Multiplied by the ten people in the room and we are rapidly in the millions! By comparison £15,000 is hardly a scratch on the surface.

And I still close 80% of the deals I set out to sell.

Listen again PLEASE.

This is what I DO. I am in my fifties and I still do it.

The ONLY people who tell me these techniques are "old-hat" and ineffective are people who don't do it … and don't even attempt to do it.

4. Excuses. Sometimes (a lot more times than you should) you are going to find yourself dealing with a prevaricating prospect. The person will express extreme keenness to take your product but will present a never ending list of issues which require resolution. You use all the techniques at your disposal to minimize and banish the usual objections but there's still "something". "The price" "The length of contract" The size (too big, too small) and so on. This is often the moment for the introduction of the, "If … then" technique. "*If … then*" is a way of "hypothetically" removing an issue which may be a smoke-screen which a non-decision maker may wish to hide behind.

Let's say the issue is the fact that your prospect regards your price as too high. So to apply "If … then", you say, "Mr. Prospect the price is clearly an issue here. **If** I was able to show you a way to overcome this hurdle **then** would you be able to proceed with this project?"

The very *idea* that a previously insurmountable barrier might be on the verge of vanishing, is often enough to spur your prospective customer into action. If he is a "pretender" (a person not able to make a final decision) then you will frequently find another, hitherto unmentioned, objection grows in its place. If this happens the best reply, to ascertain who really makes the decision (and build up your *pretender* a bit) is to say, "Mr. Prospect as there are clearly still a few things we have to address could you tell me who will be joining you in making this decision? Then we can all sit down and discuss all the issues together if you think that would be good idea."

On the other hand, if they are the real decision maker, you will find, when you ask your "If … then", that they will ask you to enlarge on your proposal immediately. One way or another you now know this IS an issue and you are talking to the right person.

Summary

Easily 80 % of sales objections are caused by Amateur Sellers talking too much about Features and Advantages in which the customer has expressed NO interest.

The four classes of objection you may still come up against are:

1. **We do**. Answer with a series of questions to establish the importance of the problem.

2. **We don't**. Answer with AIM: Acknowledge the issue, Isolate the problem, Minimize the impact, by getting your customer to concentrate on all the benefits which they have already said would be useful.

3. **How much?** Don't collapse and give discounts. Amateurs always do. Act confident. Say: "Yes, we are not the cheapest." Ask why they think so; act shocked and request some explanation. Slice your price into small bite sized sections.

4. **Excuses**. Flush-out junior "decision makers" using the "if ... then" technique. The introduction of hypothetical scenarios which appear to be on the verge of removing barriers to a sale often forces a smokescreen off the table. It is then possible to use the moment to ascertain where the decision is really being made.

6

How to sell in the worst of times

Roy, just talk nicely and she'll come out.

We've had "nice talking!" ... Now we're gonna have
"door breaking!"

WALTER MATTHAU AND LEE GRANT,
IN THE COMEDY MOVIE *PLAZA SUITE*

Things don't stay "nice" for ever. Most amateur sellers don't
really understand this. They hope people will go on buying their
stuff this year just like they did last year. They pay lip-service to
"understanding" but actually they hope, when orders are not
coming in as predicted, that it is all a horrible dream. They hope
they'll wake up in the good times again. But even great market
conditions have down-cycles. Some down-cycles last for a long
time too ... then they're called, "Recessions". Recessions and
Depressions are the stuff of all markets ... including yours.

Most non-sales people struggle a bit to deal with "selling" in
those tough markets. The first reaction is usually to cut their
prices. The second reaction is to rush around to see more
and more potential customers. Or they demand that their
professional sales people do it for them. "Sales is a numbers
game," they shout (they read that in a book somewhere).

"The more customers you see the more orders you'll get! See more customers! That's the answer!"

This, "rush around and do more things" strategy, is not a bad one in *boom* times. The first few years of the 21st century were really *boom* times. But with the banking and credit crisis which hit the world in 2007 it is bound to be "not-such-great-ones" for the next few years. Selling strategies which work quite well when things are going well "all round", are not necessarily going to work well in tighter times when customers are being more "careful" with their money.

In all there are five things that non-sales people tend to try in tough market conditions:

1. *They discount their prices.*

2. *They get hooked on "hopium" and do nothing. They "hope" something will turn up.*

3. *They do less advertising* ... can't afford it!

4. *They do more advertising* ... that'll do it!

5. *They do even more presentations and sales meetings.* The more you do the more you get.

Why discounting doesn't work. I am always surprised that most non-sellers do worry so much about "price". After all, if you're a man, do you buy the cheapest razor blades? Does the availability of a price-cut make you say to yourself, "Hmm ... I have a choice of a Gillette razor at £5 or Giltedge Rasors at £1:50 for 12. A 'made in China' brand I've never heard of but sort of *look* the same as Gillette. Yes I'll buy those and save £3.50!" And if you're a lady do you buy the cheapest stockings? "Well those sheer Agent Provocateur stockings are a bit expensive but I think I'll buy those cheapo supermarket own-brand ones. They're bound to be fine. Why pay more?!"

But many of the companies and non-seller executives I work with, DO believe that prices are the main driver in their markets. Wherever a company or its senior management see themselves as a "commodity-supplier" with a product or service that looks similar to others, they think they must discount in tough times, in order to win more business. These companies often discover, just-too-late, that the reduction in their profit margin is not covered by the resultant increased sales.

As it is the "exception that proves the rule" (I've never really understood that saying) there is evidence that, in some very low priced markets, you DO have a chance of dealing with recessions by cutting your prices. But, if you're selling Bentley motor cars against Rolls Royce then there is no need to even think about it. In fact volumes of luxury items often go up in recessionary times because there are some rich folk who enjoy "flaunting" their wealth in the face of the less well to do.

But this is not the whole story.

Up-market and higher priced "quality goods and services" in general, **do** hold their prices even in the "worst of times". This is because, when conditions are "uncertain", customers seek "quality" as a defence against "risk". Quality tends to be "certain" when the *un*certainty of tough times is waiting round every corner. People (your customers) will pay your price in order to remove or reduce risk. If a customer makes a mistake in "good-times" there is plenty of money washing around to absorb it. If the customer makes a mistake in tough times, then it can cost a great deal of real money, off the thin bottom line, with no cushion to absorb it.

I recently quoted for a negotiation training programme at a large international energy company. They wanted a lot of bespoke modules and the eventual price was relatively high. (They are a regular and very good customer but the overall price we quoted was in fact higher than it had been during the "boom-times".) We entered into negotiations with the company for this particular programme as part of a whole year's programme of various courses and workshops.

Our cumulative price was high but not out of the market. The customer argued strongly for a large discount on the overall package, citing the uncertainty of the global energy markets. They expressed anxiety about a predicted "Worldwide recession". They also spoke of "due diligence" and of looking around for alternatives if we could not "do" something on the price. We "hard-balled" it and, to be fair, they agreed that our previous work for them had been rated very highly by delegates all over the world. We'd even won an "Award" from them based on this consistent high rating. They said they'd let us know in seven days.

They did. We received a long email in which we were told that we were by far the highest priced training company they had found anywhere in Europe. There were numerous references to prices quoted by some well known competitors

– all lower. It was polite but firm. We kept reading the email. The final part of the final line was the kicker: "... *nevertheless we accept your quotation and look forward to working with you in the next 12 months.*"

A couple of weeks later I asked our main contact why they had eventually chosen us (thinking [hoping?] they were going to cite our "pedagogical creativity" and "results ori-ented" methods). What he actually said was: "*Why your company? ... You don't give us any trouble.*" In other words we were the least risky option in uncertain times.

If you're selling goods and services somewhere between the middle and high end of the market, then research shows that "price cutting" and discounting is not an effective strat-egy. Proving that you represent *safety and a reduction in risk* is the key to continued sales in tough markets.

Why getting hooked on "hopium" and "doing noth-ing" doesn't work. Looking around the global market-place I think "not doing anything" and, like Charles Dickens' Mr. Micawber, "Waiting for something to turn up", is the favourite option. When things get tough ... sit down, shut your eyes and hope it will all go away. Most politicians will always tell us that times of recession are only a temporary "retrenchment"; the good times are just around the corner. The trouble is many companies are in a state of denial and the good-times actually take a bit longer to return.

During the market crash of the late 1980s many people thought that my ex-employer Reuters might go out of busi-ness. Reuters supplied and still supply most of the financial information and electronic trading systems to the professional traders and brokers of the World. If there was less trading going on, who would need the trading systems? Many of Reuters' niche-market competitors did do nothing. Many did go out of business … sometimes in less than a year. But in Reuters we had a re-think. At the end of the American Gold Rush – we thought – people didn't stop needing shovels.

So we trained our sales force to re-train all the end-users of our services in all the ways those services could help the users to lose less money in a crashing market. We showed them how some of the less obvious applications already built into their terminals, like "real time graphics" and "arbitrage-calculators" could be used to help them "hedge" in the markets. The end-users all (well "mostly") began to believe that they couldn't afford to be without the Reuters service. When the management accountants in these customer offices came round with their clipboards looking for some easy, "recessionary cost cuts", the traders told them there was no way they could afford to be without us. As a result we lost very little and many customers actually bought more services from us.

And advertising *less* doesn't work …

> Half the money I spend on advertising is wasted. The trouble is, I don't know which half.
>
> JOHN WANAMAKER: PRESIDENT OF
> WANAMAKERS DEPT STORE, CHICAGO

There is an old saying that a female can't be "a little bit pregnant". The same goes for advertising; you either decide to do it or you decide not to do it; you can't "sort-of" do it.

Yet in an effort to cut costs in a recession many managers do order a cut in advertising costs. They reduce the coverage, the frequency and duration of their current campaign compared with their previous *boom times* one. But 50% of their previous campaign doesn't give them half the results. How could it?

That's the do *less* strategy.

But advertising *more* **doesn't work either**. The do *more* strategy is at the other end of the scale.

It is built on the perception that if twice as much is spent in the *recession* than was spent in the *boom times* then twice as much biz will come in! It is true that if you are selling very low price goods (e.g. washing-up liquid, chocolate bars, ink cartridges) that more advertising does produce more sales. But if your advertising campaign is actually there to get people to call you on the phone and a sales executive (or you) has then to go and visit the customer you still have a problem. Just carrying on with the hit or miss numbers game (the more customers you see the more business you get strategy) which is partially effective (but highly inefficient) in boom times is useless in tough times. Increased sales success is not about rushing around in general during good times and it is totally useless in a recession.

It is a waste of your senior management time deciding to spend money on advertising if you and your sales staff do not have the skills (all in this book) to use in the sales meetings generated by that advertising.

The Activity Trap (this doesn't work either). I actually learnt to sell (Rank Xerox copying machines) in the first three "recessionary" years of the 1970s in a very run down part of London. I had been trained well but still needed the corners knocked off a bit. I was rushing around giving product demos to all and sundry but failing to offer any quality or risk reduction arguments to the run down business people in this run down area. I sold very little. In fact I sold just 32% of my required target. I didn't understand. I narrowly missed being kicked out. But they put me under the wing of a wise old salesman named Johnny White and he taught me what to do and I survived!

But there is still a firm belief amongst managers that it is all a numbers game. They really think that there is a direct correlation between rushing around seeing lots of people and success in selling. I remember one extremely likeable manager telling me a few years ago that all the sales training he gave his people was to walk down the street rubbing an elbow against the wall. Every time the elbow went inwards it was an indication that there was a doorway. And behind every doorway could well be a new customer!

Even Xerox in 1970 used to tell us (after ten years of boom times before I arrived) that if you were making 15 calls each week bringing in three contracts then raising that to the company target of 25 calls a week would bring in five contracts! (Stands to reason!) Err? Well not exactly ... even the experts had to admit that. However there was certainly a bigger chance of selling more if you saw more people.

We sales people of Xerox South London (Croydon) branch circa 1970–72 were "beaten" and chased, monitored and threatened to ensure that we made the requisite number of daily sales calls. It was a very basic theory and was sound in every way … except that we didn't bring in any more business. *It did not work.*

Friday May 12th 1972

I was making more calls than just about everyone else in the branch but still I wasn't producing the required results. I was lagging way behind the top performers … they even seemed to be making *less* calls than me. This made me realize that it wasn't the rushing around that was the secret to selling in a recession (or otherwise). It must be something they were doing or saying when in front of the customer.

As we were all required to fill in activity reports I asked the local manager (a great man named Bruce Cantle (if you're still alive "Hi Bruce and thank you") to compare the activity rates of the top and bottom performers in our monthly sales meeting in Croydon's Conservative Club. He was surprised by the results and asked the top performing salesman (who had the lowest call rate of all) to present the REAL secret of sales success. He told us it was in the *questions* he asked the prospects more than anything else. The same questioning model that I've presented in this book.

All the top performers agreed with this view and I determined (on Friday May 12th 1972) to follow what they were doing. I have never looked back.

In my subsequent experience as a sales executive and trainer of sales people there are a couple of instances in which increased activity *has* produced more business. The first is where a company has recruited a large sales force in comparison to the size of the potential market. This is known as *saturation selling.*

This is quite effective for the rapid roll-out of that rare thing; a truly "unique" and desirable product. If they *have* that thing, then they can afford the luxury of a large sales force rushing around grabbing all the easy low hanging fruit. (Xerox in the mid 1960s with its first and [back then] *unique* copier, printing on to "plain paper" was one of these rarities.) But, there are only a very few sales forces that can afford such a luxury. For the vast majority of companies the market they're selling into is finite and rushing around doing "busy-work" is not likely to achieve the hoped for results.

The other instance where seeing lots of prospects or walking down the street rubbing your elbow against the wall feeling for doorways (behind which there maybe a customer) is an effective sales strategy, when your product is very inexpensive.

I am old enough to remember the "BetterWare" man of the 1950s (one of a whole UK country-wide army of "BetterWare" men) who used to call monthly at my mother's front door. This was still a time of post war rationing, so there wasn't much money about. They all had a suitcase packed with polishes, dusters, brushes and soaps of all kinds. They knocked at every domestic front door in the land – every month. My mum seemed to buy something every other time he called and the man was gone in minutes. He must have made 20 calls an hour which probably made it 100 calls a day and 500 a week. Always cheery always enthusiastic, our "BetterWare" man must have done reasonably well – provided he saw enough housewives every day. Had this man had to also sell vacuum cleaners, electric steam irons and hair-dryers the length of each call would have grown. And you can't sell a new one every week. And had he then upgraded to Dyson equipment and washing machines the whole high-activity strategy would have collapsed.

The reason that high activity strategies don't work in high priced, complex-goods markets is not clear to some non-sales people. "The harder you work the luckier you get" is a common phrase trotted out by many managing directors doing their annual "ra-ra" speech at the company sales conference. But research show us that there are many downsides to the strategy and quite a few hidden knock-on effects and it is these that contribute to the mediocre track-record of most companies in which the seniors tell their sales forces to just see a lot more customers to pull themselves out of the recessionary hole.

The management of "activity" as the panacea which will bring about increased sales actually has the following as some undesirable side effects:

- Lots of tiddly sales.
- Low levels of field coaching.
- Useless reporting systems.
- Emphasis on the "Close".

Lots of "tiddly" sales. Maybe you're different from me but I like an easy life. I don't want to rush around if I can achieve the same result, or better, by not rushing around. As my old sales manager (Bruce Cantle) used to say, "It is just as easy to sell a Mini as it is to sell a Rolls Royce".

But when you're rushing around just "seeing lots of people" with this as your primary goal, the net result tends to be the smaller more "tiddly" sale. It is easy for your sales force, if you have decreed that they must see more people, to nip round quickly and pop-in "on the off chance" at smaller, low risk and low potential prospective customers. If this is your current "recession" strategy then the effect of your "edict" is that your sellers are actually being discouraged from seeing the larger accounts. The accounts where they still have a cushion of money which they could and would spend with you, if your sales force (or YOU) presented ways in which risk and uncertainty could be reduced.

If your current activity goal is that it's all hands to the pump: OK off we go then! Everyone will see five prospects each week and from that get two "demos" and from that one sale each week ... that's the metrics we're going to measure. BEGIN! Your sales force (and YOU) will all be aiming at putting those numbers on the Big White Board in the sales office ... and the easiest way to get those numbers is what you'll all go for – tiddly "easy" accounts.

And it gets worse.

Your big accounts (oil companies, banks, manufacturers, aeroplane makers, global computer companies – all the BIG names who still have MONEY) suddenly notice that you have little time for them any more. They notice that you are treating them with an apparent lack of care. They don't realize it's all part of your desperate survival strategy and really they don't care. And if there are two things people and large companies crave it is care and attention.

> Everybody loves flattery … with Royalty you lay it
> on with a trowel.
>
> BENJAMIN DISRAELI: UK PRIME MINISTER IN THE REIGN OF
> QUEEN VICTORIA

Low levels of field coaching. All the textbooks on management tell you this (and it's even in my airport bookshop favourite, *The One Minute Manager* by Ken Blanchard) the most effective activity of excellent man-managers is that of "coaching".

By "coaching" I mean you (or your sales management experts) spending time in the field observing and advising sales people on their customer facing behaviours. The effective behaviours are the ones outlined in this book … especially those that focus on the power and skill of questioning.

If you or your sales-managers are out there rushing around with the rest of "the guys" and endeavouring to close business you won't be doing the coaching. And in tough times coaching and training are sidelined in order to ensure that everyone sees more customers. Yet research shows that reinforcing those effective anti-recessionary behaviours with regular coaching gives your sales people confidence. It increases morale. They are (unusually) being given feedback on what they are doing right (most managers see their role as catching their staff doing things wrong). When they start doing the right things in a recessionary environment the transformation is rapid. Large well-heeled accounts begin to hear what they want to hear and feel they are being "attended to". They begin to order more Rolls Royces and fewer Minis and all for less effort on your part.

Useless reporting systems. Between 1973 and 1975 and in a recession, I sold an industrial catering service for a company in South East London. The new sales manager was a numbers man. Oh yes, he loved his numbers and reporting systems. He even made them into a graph charting activity against sales and the line went diagonally from the top corner to the bottom ... downwards. He brought the graph to a sales meeting mounted on a large piece of art-board. Lots of carefully chosen primary colours proved we were all useless. He was a "cross" and "angry" sales manager at that meeting ... that is until somebody pointed out that the graph he was showing us was upside down.

I don't think there is anything wrong in getting sales people to let management know what they're up to on a daily basis. Call reports are part of a professional sales executive's life. Provided the information is read properly (and the right way up) and analysed for more than: how many customers did you see today, this week, this month; then they do no harm.

It all starts to go wrong when a sales person in a "tough market" is asked to spend more and more time accounting for their daily activity. According to my own observations and speaking to my old sales colleagues across many companies and banks in the USA and the UK, I have discovered that the need to report and maintain accurate activity records does indeed increase in recessionary times.

Looking back to 1973, 1987, 1992 all periods of tough market conditions, this is how the need for activity reporting increased in those tough markets across a total of 39 organizations:

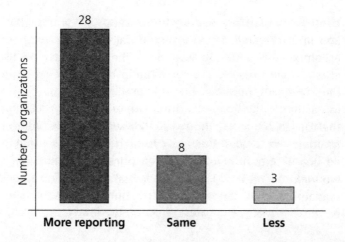

Also just like me they had all found that they were involved (as the title of the old John Cleese management training film suggests) in more "Meetings ... Bloody Meetings". All of those meetings were for sales management people like me to explain to my bosses why sales were so abysmal.

As things got worse I was spending more time in HQ with the CEO, COO and CIO (explaining things for them to relay to the MD) and less time in the field coaching my sales people. My original 1970 sales manager, Bruce Cantle used to say that if a company is constantly calling sales people out of the field to explain things to everyone else inside HQ then it is not a particularly healthy place to be – business wise. The more trees that were cut down to make paper to record what was going on rather than getting out there to fix it, the worse things were getting.

Emphasis on the Close. As the easiest person to pick on from a senior point of view is the sales manager they are often the only person seen by the guys upstairs and the person on whom all the pressure is placed to close more business. The panic stricken sales manager then rushes around trying to close things himself. He tells everyone in the sales team that he will accompany the Closings. (Oh no … not him … he's a nightmare … when did he last sell anything?) The management activity is focused on sales visits at an advanced stage of the sales cycle where the sale is due to be "born" any moment now. The opening of the cycle is ignored and yet all the evidence is that the opening stages of a sale is when the management (not just sales management) can have the greatest effect on the final result.

Why? … easy. If you mess up the opening stages of a sale there will be no Close. As you know from your computer programming basic training it's RIRO (Rubbish In Rubbish Out) that governs the whole thing, so it is with selling. Get the opening right and the close will happen by itself without your help (more often than not).

> Morale in this company has always been "at an all time low".
>
> BRUCE CANTLE: MY RANK XEROX SALES MANAGER IN 1973

So what *does* bring in sales in the worst of times?

I have set out as simply as I can all the things that Amateur Sellers typically do when the going gets tough. I'm not an academic so I hope my simple explanations have made clear why they are not, in my experience, particularly effective strategies. My most successful customers, from a sales training point of view, are those who have grasped three important ideas and acted on them:

1. **Coach at the coal face.** Shouting and screaming and sending down Snottagrams* or walking around giving out high-five palm-slaps and shouting "We're winning!" at every opportunity (when we're clearly not) doesn't fix much. You (the manager), or your sales managers, need to ensure that the correct, validated and researched behaviours are being used in all customer facing situations. If they (your sales team) are all carrying on with the rushing-around strategies which "sort-of" worked in the *boom times* you are NOT going to get the results you need in the tough times.

2. **Technique not hysteria.** There is a story of a young adolescent male lion standing on a rock next to the King of the Pride looking down on a large group of young females who have suddenly come into view. "Quick," he says excitedly to the older male. "Let's rush down as fast as we can and each mate with one of those females!" "No", says the King. "Let us rather walk down slowly and mate with all of them!"

If you or your professional sellers are not getting sales in boom times or tough times, it is because you, or they, are not doing the right things. Seeing more customers and then doing the wrong things when you're with them, is not particularly helpful. You must work on the skills which are proven to be effective when you are facing your customer.

---

*An ancient expression meaning nasty, sarcastic management note.

3. Slick tyres for dry tracks. If a "Formula 1" racing driver was to drive on to a wet racing circuit with the same smooth, treadless-tyres he used on a hot dry track he would skid out of control in seconds. It is also very inefficient to keep deep-tread rain tyres which reduce road-contact surface area on the car on a hot dry day. And it's the same with selling. You cannot use the same skills in tough times that you were using when the sun was shining. It is a great pity that so many organizations are still teaching their sales people to sell in the same confrontational way, with call rate the number one objective.

These "activity" methods were developed in the less sophisticated markets of the 1960s; they are not for today.

Summary

When markets get difficult, and ALL markets get tough sometimes, there are things to avoid and things to DO.

There is no evidence that reducing your price will bring you more business.

There is no evidence that just sitting there "hooked on hopium" will bring you more business.

There is no evidence that rushing around banging on more doors improves your business.

There is no evidence that doing more or less advertising will improve your business.

The answer is to use the material in this book. Prepare more. Use what you now know to create value in your customer's mind. Know what problems your product is designed to fix and get your prospective customer to think about them. If you are a senior manager then coach more in the field. If you can't coach your sales people yourself make sure that your sales managers have the time and mandate from you to coach more.

7

Getting your contract signed

In most conjuring tricks the "trick" is executed
by the magician at the start.
The magician's art is then to make the audience
forget what he did back then.
The miraculous event then just *happens* at the end.

JOSEPH DUNNINGER: MAGICIAN

I am not a New Age seller who is attempting to tell you that
"sales just happen". You say a few words over your prospective customer ... ask a few Worry Questions ... increase the
pain ... do a demonstration or presentation and the customer
begs you to let them have your product or service at any price.
It happens ... sometimes ... rarely ... but it does happen.

The more common situation requires that you learn to hold
your customer's hand (in a purely metaphorical sense!) and
confidently take them where the grass is green and your product or service is just waiting to help them out of their misery.

The method I recommend is that you see the sales process
as a series of steps. You should not embark on a sales meeting unless you can write down on a piece of paper
beforehand, exactly what you want the next meeting to
achieve. And the next one. And the next one.

The good news is that most amateur and inexperienced sellers (your competitors) don't do this. They are hooked on "Hopium" here as well as at other stages of the sale. They regard selling as a spinning Roulette wheel which may or may not give them what they want. They "hope" Lady Luck will smile on them. Their fortune is in the lap of the Gods ... toss fate to the wind every time.

Do you get a feeling of déjà vu here ? The more people you see the more orders you get? Throw enough mud at the wall and some of it is bound to stick? STOP ... have you learnt nothing from this little gold mine of a book? I spent 37 years in the "school of hard knocks" to provide you with this "inside knowledge". You have more control of things in selling than a gambling wheel IF you follow the techniques I am about to lay in front of you.

Are you listening?

People are hard to "persuade" so you have to get them to *persuade* themselves (that's where all that questioning skill comes in). But human brains are very easy to "Influence" and that is what I am going to show you here in the next few pages. Take no notice of the nay-sayers who will tell you this stuff doesn't work ... I use it all the time and it does ... even in the 21st century!

Firstly the shape of a sale looks something like this:

Sixth meeting
Objective: get the contract
signed
Next step: get meeting with
adjacent department head

Fifth meeting
Objective: remove FDs
anxieties
Next step: finalize the sale

Fourth meeting
Objective: present the proposal
Next step: discuss with their
Finance Director

Third meeting
Objective: present a solution
Next step: present a proposal

Second meeting
Objective: to investigate more
problem areas
Next step: present a possible
solution

First meeting
Objective: is this an
opportunity?
Next step: meet his boss

The "Next Step" model

The sales process may actually go on for ten meetings or
twenty meetings or more with your prospect. But the idea at
each stage is that YOU **must** have an objective for each

meeting and a minimum acceptable "Next Step" in your mind. The surprising thing is that so many Amateur Sellers do not have any objective or goal in mind for the impending meeting with a client let alone thinking ahead to the one after that!

The reason it is so important is that making a "decision" is a worry to most human beings. They are loaded with anxiety. Don't believe me? Stand behind someone in line at Burger King or McDonalds. They get to the front of the line ... right up against the counter THEN they look up at the illuminated menu above the servers. "What shall I have? What shall I have? It's all so confusing! I *was* going to have a Double Whammy Burger with fries and a Coke but now ... I don't know." (They've been staring up at the menu for five minutes waiting in line ... and they still don't know!) "I think I'll have ... No ... instead a fish burger and salad ... or a simple burger and fries ... no wait a minute ..."

If the server was to say, "May I make a suggestion? The Double Whammy Burger is on special offer today with free fries and a half price Coke. I suggest that as your best choice as a delicious and cost effective meal." Then most of the adult population of the Western world would gratefully accept this decision-made-for-them.

Your task as a confident and apparently professional seller is to ask questions in a chatty manner during the meeting and then tell the prospect what the next step should be and get them to commit to it. Before taking each "Next Step" you must know both the objective of the meeting and your minimum acceptable "Next Step" after that. Usually, when I ask an Amateur Salesperson to tell me the objective of a sales meeting they have set up, they tell me, "To get a contract signed of course ... errr ... if I can". Is that what YOU say? Is that what you *would* say? Oh dear! Then (if YOU are the "Amateur Seller" I've just asked), YOU are going to be very disappointed as you walk out of 90% of your prospective customer meetings.

The reality of the sales process is that, unless your product is very inexpensive, it is probably going to take several steps (meetings) to get the prospect to "sign on the dotted line". Taking "selling" as a general subject, I would say that the chance of you getting the "Yes" you are seeking each time is about **10%** averaged over all your genuine sales meetings. People, (your customers) usually take their time over saying, "Yes". (If you read my book *Negotiating Skills for Virgins* you will learn that to make the other side wait, and invest their time, as long as possible, is a matter of effective strategic planning for top negotiators.)

But equally most people also take their time over giving you an outright "No" as well. Once again the chance of you hearing your prospect say a final "No" is also only about **10%**.

So here's the interesting dilemma.

If they are only likely to tell you **"Yes" 10% of the time** and only likely to tell you **"No" 10 % of the time** ... what is happening the other **80% of the time** at the end of an average customer sales meeting?

Yes ... it's "Limbo" time!

Somewhere between Heaven and Hell, according to some religious experts, is a place called "Limbo". It is neither one thing nor the other. It is a waiting area around which lost souls wander whilst they await their eternal fate. They haven't been sent down below but neither have they been allowed into Paradise. *It is where most Amateur Sellers spend **80%** of their time.* Most Sales Forecasts consist of hundreds of any-moment-now sales in this "80% Limbo".

"Sales Limbo", from the point of view of an Amateur Sales executive, is a "place in time" where it is far too early to give up hope and "call-it-a-day" and yet … the contract isn't signed yet either. In the words of the song (slightly paraphrased) the customer hasn't said, "yes" and they haven't said, "no". They haven't said, "stay" and they haven't said, "go".

The way to know whether you have entered "Sales Limbo" is to listen out for these phrases from your prospective customers:

- We'll let you know soon.
- That was a great presentation … we'll be in touch.
- You are one hell of a salesman … we'll have a think and then I'll ring you.
- We really like what you've shown us … we just need to go over the numbers then we'll call you.
- Give us a few days to discuss it then I'll get back to you.
- When we have read your proposal I'll call you.
- We'll definitely be in touch.
- Give us a couple of weeks to mull it over and then I'll get my secretary to arrange another appointment.
- This is extremely interesting … I'm definitely on your side on this. Just give us a couple of days and I'll give you a ring.
- I just need to get the nod from "the-powers-that-be" upstairs, then I'll be able to give you the go-ahead.

- Thank you for responding to our RFQ (Request For Quotation document). Once we have read your submission and those from all the other vendors, we will be in touch again. Talk to you soon ... Goodbye.

ALL these jolly optimistic phrases are all signs that you are entering, or have already entered, "Sales Limbo" – a place ruled over by polite, non-confrontational people who I'm sure make up the majority of your customers. (They make up the majority of mine anyway). They don't want to upset you or risk a confrontation should they say directly, "actually your product is not for us", or "thank you for your submission but we have chosen another supplier". Because they believe you (with all your undoubted clever sales executive's slick-objection-rebuttal-skills) will enter into some clever verbal fisticuffs. Some sort of imagined "word-play" which "top sellers" are taught that might make them feel awkward and unable to defend their decision not to use your company. Anything to avoid confrontation!

Instead they are polite ... they say things they think you want to hear like: "You're a great sales person!" "That is one fantastic product you have there!" "We'll call you soon ... we will!" What you are actually hearing is a translation of: "We're not sure" "We're not convinced yet" "We can probably manage without it" "I dunno!" This is the way polite people speak.

Your job, on the other hand, is to remove your Amateur Seller's hat and, instead, don your brilliantly trained Professional Seller's "Mortarboard". Because you know that, unless you stay "in control" of this situation, the hunger and desire for your solution, on the part of your customer, will quickly dissipate. And I'll tell you what will happen if you walk out now with a "Limbo phrase" ringing in your ears; a competitor who has read this book will nip in and pinch your business.

A competitor just like me.

The "Next Step" strategy

But today I am here to help you. You are now leaving "Limbo" for all of Eternity. You will never return again. From now on you will always have a good handle on where you really stand with each customer at each step of the sale. You are not going to be pushy in the old-fashioned sense, just confident, assured and efficient. You are going to use one of the powerful and immutable Laws of Influence. These are not New Age get-rich-quick Laws of the Universe (e.g. the Immutable Law of Money, the Universal Law of Attraction) but academically researched, measurable and repeatable patterns of human behaviour. The one you are about to be introduced to is known as the "Law of Commitment and Consistency".

In his 2003 book *Influence,* Professor Robert Cialdini of Arizona State University states that there are six basic laws by which humans can be influenced to do things which we might otherwise resist. The Laws are called: "Reciprocity", "Authority", "Commitment and Consistency", "Social Proof", "Scarcity" and "Likeability". Each law is described and illustrated with ample proofs throughout his book, which I recommend you read as soon as you can. It is fascinating, very powerful and in some areas quite alarming. Nevertheless the only one of these laws we have space for in this book is the law of "Commitment and Consistency".

The basic tenet of this law is that if a human being commits publicly to doing something, that person is 80%

more likely to do it. By "publicly" I mean: "tells at least one other person", that they definitely will do something. This "Law of Commitment" is especially strong if the person ties their commitment to a particular date and time. The reason for its effectiveness seems to be that we all have a deep need to be seen by others as cooperative and reliable. In order for ancient tribal groups to function effectively, members of the group had to know they could rely on each other. To tell another you would do something and then fail could result in your unguarded village being attacked, your neighbour's house being robbed, your side in a battle being unsupported during an attack.

So, before you leave your office for any sales meeting, you MUST be able to articulate the *minimum* "Next Step" that you are going to get the prospective customer to take. You MAY be fortunate and discover during the meeting that you are able to take a much bigger step with the customer; be ready. Nobody on the planet knows what is going to happen next. (Who was it said, "The only thing we humans can be sure of is Death and Taxes?")

The "Next Step" is simply a proven and validated way to use human psychology to keep as much control of the sales process as is humanly possible. (And that's 80% more control than most "Amateurs".) A typical Next Step will sound like this:

"So, the next step is to give you and your team a demonstration of our product and show you how it will address your issues. I can do next Friday at 10.15 or Monday at 15.30. Which is best for you?" (Notice the date and time – YOU suggest it. Don't wait for the customer!)

Or: "What would you suggest as the best next action? Should we see the CEO first or should the Chief Trader be next so that we can show them what we are discussing?" "The CEO is best I think," says the customer. You reply, "Right, all we have to do is get this in our diaries when we can all find 20 minutes. I can do any afternoon next week or Monday or Tuesday morning. Could we give him a call so that we know which is best for him then we can fix it all up?"

Or: "OK if that proposal accurately reflects the solution you're looking for, we really need to make sure your Finance Director is on board. If we could give his PA a call we can get something in his diary to discuss this proposal. I'd suggest next Wednesday or Friday. Which one should we aim for? Friday?

Or: "So you'll see the Technical Manager yourself tomorrow ... that's great! And so, I'll book our survey team now for Friday so that we can get them to look over the site before installation starts. When's a good time for you on Friday, am or pm?"

Or: "When is a good time for me to bring in the proposal* and go through it with you? Next Thursday or ... the following Tuesday?"

So, *every* time ... at the end of *every* prospect meeting ... to turn that final "Limbo" moment (So what would you like to do now, Mr Prospect?) into a "Next Step" (This is what we're going to do), suggest the next step and endeavour to confidently hang a date and time on it which your customer agrees. And decide what that minimum next step is going to be before you go in to see the customer.

---

*Never *send* a proposal! ... take it in yourself and go through it with your prospect.

Will your prospect ALWAYS do what you suggest? Of course not but *they will do 80% of the time*. You will find that other human beings LOVE anyone who seems to know what to do next in life. Always sound confident at the Next Step!

YES ... there will finally be a time to "Close" the sale

The moment of the "Close" is often regarded as THE moment of the sale. Many managers want to be "there" when the sale is being consummated. They believe that is their "moment". The moment when they can be of most value to the sales process. (The moment when they can gain the most kudos from their own boss for their brilliant management of the process? Perish the thought!) The point at which the customer finally decides, irrevocably, to spend the money. Well "Yes" and "No".

People in social interactions of all types (business and pleasure) do make decisions about other people very early on. Calculating how to respond to other humans in every type of social setting is the time our human brains are at their most active each day.

Research shows that a woman sitting in a bar makes up her mind whether the guy who has just walked through the door is the *Alpha Male* in just **three** seconds. The ensuing "chat-up" may go on for some time ... but deep in her heart the decision: "would I get into bed with him?" has already been made. And in business too, the customer has been making their mind up for a long time before the "Close".

We used to be told in Rank Xerox (my sales birthplace) that a customer actually makes up their mind whether they will do business with you at the very first meeting. And in the first part of that first meeting ... in the first 15 seconds it takes you to walk across his carpet from the office door to his desk.

So "Closing" your sale is *important*, but not MORE important than anything else in this book. (Actually, if there was one activity I would have to select which makes all the difference to you, as a newly graduated Professional Persuader, it is *questioning*, which is why there is so much about it in this book).

When your customer has been encouraged to discuss all the worries, wants, needs and concerns at length. When you have nudged them "Next Step" by "Next Step" towards the final solution. When you have presented your proposal and got everybody on-board who needs to be on-board, there will probably be a need for you to say something.

True, the customer may well say to you, "OK let's get this show on the road! Where do I sign?" But equally they may not. They may just sit there saying to themselves:

Well is that all the bases covered? Yes I think so... but IS this the right thing to do?

Am I making the right decision? It IS a lot of money after all ... on the other hand the cost of not doing anything is higher.

But ON the other hand we've managed alright without a solution so far? ... I dunno ... perhaps ...

This is the moment YOU come to the rescue!

You are **Decision Man**   You are **Deciding Woman**

> If the trumpet sounds an *uncertain* note then who will ride into battle?
>
> ANON

You have already seen in this book that people *hate* making decisions.

DECIDE! On the flight deck of modern passenger carrying airliners they know this too. So they force the crew on the flight deck to make them.

On a long low-visibility "instrument landing" into a misty, fog-bound airport one of the flight crew will be flying the plane and the other will be monitoring the instruments. These instruments tell the pilot how far off the centre line of the runway the plane is, how fast it is going, how high above the ground and how far from the runway threshold. They may be able to see nothing out of the window … just grey mist. They are concentrating on keeping the two cross-hairs of the landing instrument ("centre-line" and "glide-slope") steadily crossed in the middle of the instrument panel.

The co-pilot constantly reads, out loud, other instrument readings for the benefit of the pilot. When the co-pilot reaches the latest possible "minimum decision" point (hundreds of feet above the ground, distance from the runway etc) they will tell the pilot, "You are on the centre line ... 180 knots ... 500 feet above the runway and 2000 feet from the threshold ... DECIDE!"

The pilot cannot say, "Errr ... I dunno". There are only two pre-scribed answers. They must say either: "LAND" or "ABORT".

And immediately, depending on that decision, a different set of procedures is locked in. If it's "LAND" then they do the final pre landing checks and trust that the runway lights will show up pretty fast! One way or another they ARE going to land! If it's "ABORT" then it's full power, nose-up and climb-away fly round "the circuit", line-up again and prepare for another attempt. No pilot ever lost points for "going around".

In a sale it is not quite as black and white.

You won't be saying to your customer, after your own "long slow approach", "DECIDE!" But if you don't do something NOW I have seen many great sales dwindle to nothing and go completely "cold". But you will be making the decision much easier for him to make NOW. For this purpose there exists a variety of quite innocuous closing techniques which will not strike your prospective customer as "pushy" but nevertheless are remarkably powerful decision influencers.

The first one is called the Alternative Close.

The alternative close

It is a strange little trait of the human brain that, if you offer it a choice of two options under almost any circumstances, it will tend to select one of them.

In a shoe shop, for example, a properly trained shop assistant will only ever have two pairs of shoes open in front of
you at any one time. Any more than that and customers
tend to get confused and say, "Well ... I dunno!" On the
other hand, if there's only one pair open, customers tend to
say, "Mmm ... I think I'll have a look next door to see what
they have. Thanks anyway!" With the two choice "alternative" option the sales assistant simply says, "They both suit
you madam. Which one do YOU prefer, the brown shoes or
the black shoes?" If they ask that question then, all the available research shows that, 80% of the time, the customer will
select one of the pairs. You may even get lucky (10% of the
time) and sell both pairs! Or you may (also about 10% of the
time) hear the "I think I'll try next door".

With the "alternative close" the customer perceives that they
were offered a choice and therefore were not pushed into a
sale. The final decision was theirs, so ... no argument ... a
rational choice was made. It always seems to escape people
that there was no real YES or NO choice. Both choices were
a YES to go ahead with you.

So look at your product or service. What alternatives can you
offer?

The one year contract or the two year?

The large earth digger or the small one?

The Plasma Flat Screen or the LCD Flat Screen?

The complete frontal restoration or just the upper set?

A print run with the plasticized finish or the matt finish?

The pay-as-you-go option or the six month pre-pay contract?

How would you like to pay … cash or credit card?

The minor point close

A close ally of the Alternative Close is the "Minor Point Close". This is an especially effective tool when you are selling high value items. No customer (including me) wants to feel that they are having to make a decision to spend a lot of money to buy a house or a car for example. We put it off. We tend to go into "mañana" mode. (Tomorrow will do.) Help me somebody … tell me what to do … make it easy.

The professional sellers of high value goods and services know this, so they make it easy … still leaving you feeling that you made a "Man's" decision. They get you to make an alternative choice but on a minor point. They say:

"Well it's as simple as this… do you prefer the red one or the silver one?" [Jaguar car that is … retailing at $90,000] *Colours*? Minor decision.

"You can have this airplane with either five seats and extra luggage space or six seats and a table. Which option is going to be the best for you? You can always alter it quickly later on? Which version would you prefer us to fit first?" [Partenavia twin-prop aircraft that is … retailing at $700,000.] *Number of Seats*? Minor decision.

"OK just to summarize: the information system for your Dealing Room will cover all 500 trading positions and offer real-time foreign exchange rates securities and news. The contract is for two years and the only thing to sort out now is whether you want the training to be carried out in our training school or would you like our trainers to come here? There's no extra charge either way." [A complete information and trading system, tied up for two years on a rolling contract. Licence for all 500 positions: $500,000 per month.] *Training here or there*? Minor decision.

It isn't only alternatives either. Sometimes the "Continuous Assumptive Close" just slots right in.

The continuous assumptive close*

Sometimes you're chatting to the decision maker and you suddenly get the feeling that a written proposal isn't going to be necessary. (Could you, maybe, jump the planned Next Step? Could you jump three Next Steps!?) There's something in the way he's speaking that suggests he is very keen. Introduce a Continuous Assumptive Close and see what happens.

Let's see ... change the language to an "assumptive" tone. Not: "**if** you implement our training programme", but, "**when** you implement it". Not, "you **could** see a big change in the negotiating skills of your team", but "your delegates **will** discover a big change in their negotiating ability once they've been through the programme". Then hang a simple question on the end, "So when I get back, I'll just get the workbooks compiled for you and off we go. I think you said the first week in January was probably the right time for you, which is fine for us too. I'm really looking forward to working with you on this."

---

*Please don't tell me this doesn't work. I've just used it today, in London in 2007, to secure for my own company, a one-year training contract against two national competitors!

Sometimes you will find you are up against a real street-fighter. Especially if your main contact has (as one of your final Next Steps) introduced you to the founding CEO of the company for their "final blessing". They've seen all the proposals and they want you (Mr. so-called "Salesman"!) to know that THEY are the big shot round here and they want what THEY want!

Congratulations! You are up against the Classic "Driver" personality ... assertive, confrontational and slightly intimidating. As examples, look at well known public figures like Alan Sugar (CEO – Amstrad), Donald Trump (US property tycoon), John Prescott (Labour Party MP), and the late Lord King (MD – British Airways).

In this case, whatever you do, they will want something different. You say "black" they'll say "white". You say "big" they'll say "small". And vice versa, all the way down the line. The really *great* thing about these "DRIVERS" is that they make quick decisions. You don't have to use a Minor Point Close because they are familiar with handling and dealing with very large amounts of money. They are used to it! What they will do, however, is endeavour to "knock you down" because they are professional wheeler dealers and ... well ... that's what they DO.

So in these cases your strategy is simple; it is the "Contrast Close".

The contrast close

This "close" is used a lot in retail and all you will be doing is adapting it for use in your own sales arsenal. It is best explained by an example. Let us say that you are buying your winter wardrobe and you urgently need two items of clothing: a "winter overcoat" and a "sweater". You are browsing in the coats department in a large store and the sales assistant approaches you. "Good morning ... How can I help?" "Yes thank you. I'm looking for a new overcoat and a new wool sweater."

Now here's the question ... which one is the sales assistant (if they have been well trained) going to try to sell you first? Did you answer, "The overcoat"? Good, nothing very difficult there. Of course they will try and sell you the higher priced item first.

But there's another reason too. If they have been able to sell you the higher priced coat it is relatively easy to sell you a high priced additional item. The reason is that, having spent say £190 (USD $380 approx) on the coat, you will be much more amenable to buying a high priced sweater for £85 (USD $160 approx). This is because having spent so much on a coat the lower priced sweater (even though it is actually quite expensive) feels psychologically easily affordable by comparison.

Shoe shops always do it. You buy a pair of shoes £120 (USD $210 approx) and what do they say when you present yourself at the payment counter? "Would you like some black shoe polish for your new shoes today?" "Oh yes," you say. [Thinking of the dried-up tin you opened yesterday morning] Good idea. Put a tin in the bag ... that's fine ... thanks." You hand over your credit card ... and sign the voucher or enter your PIN. You don't notice that the total is now £124 (USD $217). You have just paid twice the price – or more – for a tin of ordinary shoe polish than you would have paid in your local supermarket. But compared with the comparatively large amount you've just paid for the shoes ... well ... the price of the shoe polish seems "trifling" by comparison.

This business of decision influencing is very strange and always "comparative". You see an electronic calculator on sale in your local stationery store for £20 but there's a sign on it telling you that tomorrow – as it's a Bank Holiday – there will be a special store wide **"25% off day"**. If you wait a day you could buy the same calculator for just £15! (Save £5!) Would you leave it and come back in the morning ... 80 % of people would ... why pay more?

Different scenario: what about you needing a new Personal Computer? The one you want is available for £300 (USD $600 approx) but there's a sign on it telling you that as it's a Bank Holiday tomorrow there's a store wide £5 (USD $9 approx) off everything. Would you buy it now or come back tomorrow ... 80% of people wouldn't wait to save that amount of money on an expensive computer. And yet ... the amount of money saved in both cases is identical!

The difference is in the customer's perception of comparative relativity. (I made that phrase up, but you know what I mean.)

So when you're up against a "Driver" you can use exactly the same method. He will ask you (gruffly) how much all this is going to cost him ... even though you've been over it twenty times with his staff. Make sure that you say, confidently, whatever the biggest order you can imagine in your wildest dreams would cost, for example: "To deliver this to all 100 of your traders will cost $1,000,000 over two years." OR: "To purchase all 12 of these trucks the total price will be £240,000." OR: "To run five of these 20 day negotiating training programmes for you over the next two years comes to a total of £700,000."

In each case, the deal you had been discussing until you first met the "Driver" (20 minutes ago) was much less than the numbers you have just given him. Only 50 traders were going to be using the service at first; only eight trucks were in the original proposal; only three negotiation programmes were under discussion at present.

"WHAT!?" the Driver will say. "That's a hell of a lot of money! No ... no ... no, we're going to start off with a much smaller number!" "We only need 60 of our traders on your system at the start!" "We only need 9 of these trucks ... there's still some life left in at least three of the old ones!" "No, I don't think we need to commit to five programmes at the moment we'll start with three and see how we go!"

The Driver shakes your hand and shows you the door. (I showed them who was in charge, he thinks. Oh yes ... coming in here with their big ideas ... good products maybe ... but I knocked them down ... that feels good. I won!) He doesn't realize that you (once an Amateur Seller) are standing at that moment round the corner from his office block, with your Professional Sales colleague (now two Professional Sellers side by side) firmly shaking each other by the hand. DEAL DONE! A classic "Contrast Sale".

When doing business with a Driver, the general trend is try to, "knock you down". Drivers will never "knock you UP" (in the nicest sense of the phrase). Don't say anything like, "Well Mr. Driver, I thought we'd let you see how good we are and I suggest we initially install just one [of whatever you're selling] and see how it goes." If you do that Mr. Driver will ask you for a "free trial" ... I guarantee it.

Never reduce your price when in front of a Driver because, as a general rule-of-thumb, you will end up with less!

Occasionally (yes it does happen) you will get the shock of your life when a Driver says, in reply to your full-on "Contrast Close", "WHAT? ... you're *very* expensive ... are these things gold-plated?! [long silence] but I guess we need it ... OK we'll go ahead with all 100 ... but don't you let us down on this or I'll have your guts for garters!" Your reaction at this point is to "act cool". You have just got a HUGE deal. You must act as if this happens to you every day. You must not "dribble", "foam at the mouth" or say, "cha-ching!" You smile, say "Thank you" ... get his signature on the contract, shake his hand then get out of his office. Get out of his building and off his premises. Go round the corner ... NOW go berserk!

And finally ...

There are many ways to "close" a sale but for the sake of this little gold-mine-of-a-book, I'm going to introduce you to the (so-called) "Winston Churchill Balance Sheet". In the USA they call the identical "closing" method, the "Ben Franklin Balance Sheet"; they're both identical. In both cases it was supposed to be the way these eminent gentlemen made decisions of great moment. Whether they did or not ... who knows.

The Winston Churchill balance sheet

There will be the odd time when your prospective customer is not sure. There are clearly many things making them anxious. They just can't decide. If you're not careful you will get into a long term/permanent "We'll let you know soon" loop. Something light ... but effective is required.

So reach down into your briefcase and bring out a sheet of plain white paper. Say, "There are clearly quite a few things concerning you still. Do you mind if I jot a few of them down here, just so I understand everything? [Don't wait for a reply. Place the piece of paper in "portrait" orientation in front of you and draw a line down the middle from top to bottom. Place a "+" at the top of the left column and a "–" at the top of the right column. Then continue …] So on the positive side you said you liked the [now write down, on the left, all the things the customer told you, during the investigation/questioning phase that they liked about your product … use the words and phrases they used.] The flexibility of the contract; the tailor-made modules that you said other contractors would not do for you; the fact that we will keep a full set of spares on your site so there will be no waiting for deliveries; the choice of either a 240 volt or 110 volt power supply so that you can use the equipment in USA; the fully comprehensive insurance cover for which there is no charge for the first five years … and the motorized trolley which ensures full mobility on site. On the other side … the things that you're still not sure about are …?" [Say nothing, don't prompt … wait for them.]

They say, "Well, the fact that your products don't have the paper filters we're used to … and what else? Oh yes, and you don't have a permanent office in Singapore … just a local rep … that's a bit of a concern." [Get them to write those two things on your paper on the right hand side under the "minus" sign.]

What you will usually find is that your prospect can rarely think of as many negative things against your proposition as compared with all the positive agreed "benefits and advantages" on the left. You of course derived these "positives" from the earlier questioning and investigative phases of the sales process, *which is why "questioning* rather than *"telling" is so important when you're selling.* Faced with the "hard copy" (the evidence) written down on the paper, expressed in their words, it is very compelling. Sure, there maybe a couple of negatives ... but on balance the six "benefits" really outweigh the "negs" quite strongly.

The Winston Churchill balance sheet

+	−
Contract flexibility	No paper filters
Tailor-made bespoke modules	Only a rep office in Singapore
Full set of spares on site	
Choice of 240v or 110v	
Fully comprehensive insurance – first 5 years free	
Motorized trolley for mobility	

An additional "strengthener" of the supporting evidence presented by the "Winston Churchill balance sheet" is to offer your prospect the opportunity to "weight" each one of the benefits/disadvantages with a score of between, say, 1 and 10 on both sides of the line. So the prospect will say something along the lines of: "OK I give the first benefit 'plus four', the second 'plus five', the third 'plus five', the fourth 'plus four', the fifth 'plus nine' and the last one 'plus three' ... making a total of thirty. On the other side of the line, the paper filter issue is a 'minus five' and the Singapore thing a 'minus ten' ... so that's minus fifteen!"

Then you say, "So really the evidence speaks for itself ... the benefits for you clearly outweigh the downsides. It is only really a case of deciding whether you want to take the service on the five year or the three year contract ..."

And there is one last thing you must be aware of if you are really going to be any good at this selling game: **Omerta** – at the heart of the Italian Mafia (Cosa Nostra) is a code of conduct. It is the rule of silence. You learn to say nothing.

The Law Of Silence

You know what it's like. You and your partner (husband, boyfriend, wife, girlfriend) have decided to have an argument. It has reached a particularly intense phase and right now you're actually not talking to each other! In fact you have made an irrevocable decision not to talk to the other person in your life, ever again, "so long as you both shall live" ... ever ... ever!

SILENCE REIGNS

So now that you're in this self imposed "purdah" what is the golden rule, not written in any books on relationships; never defined in any form, written or oral; not marked in any ancient texts that everyone knows but nobody ever discusses? What do we all know about, "the silence"?

Here it is:

The person who speaks first loses!

And so it is with selling. I think a golden rule of selling (one of many) should be:

NEVER MISS A GOOD OPPORTUNITY TO SHUT UP!

Silences are like a magic spell when you're endeavouring to persuade another person. When the customer goes quiet,

YOU SAY NOTHING. It really doesn't matter how long the silence goes on for.

If you've just made your "Next Step" or even your "Close" and the customer is saying nothing, then you keep your mouth closed otherwise you WILL break the spell. Silences are very persuasive things because people, particularly in the West (rather than Japan or China where polite silences are very much part of the culture), can't stand them and they will do anything to break them ... even if that means signing your contract.

If you say something daft to break the silence like: "Is everything OK, Mr. Prospect?" or "Is there anything else you need to think about, Mr. Prospect? or [worse] "You've gone very quiet, Mr. Prospect" ... then you are asking to walk out of his door with nothing.

So remember: the person who speaks first loses.

Summary

Before each meeting with a customer you must know exactly what "Next Step" you want to achieve at that meeting.

Finally, you must learn to appreciate and use some of the tried and tested "Closes" to employ at the end of the sales process. In particular the "Alternative Close" which relies on the fact that human brains respond favourably when presented with two alternative solutions to an issue. And also the "Contrast Close" which encourages you to have the courage to ask for a large order whenever you can. This is on the basis that, in business, most customers will try to drive you down; occasionally they will accept your proposal and do the large deal; but they will never try to drive you up if you request a small initial deal!

8

The ubiquitous sales letter

It was November 2007 that I began to complete this book. I was going to finish it at the last chapter. But then something happened. I received a sales letter. It was from an Estate Agent offering to sell my London apartment (if I wanted to). It was such an awful letter but so true to type (and absolutely useless as a selling tool) that I decided to add this brief section on writing a sales letter. I realized that without it, the book you have in your hands would be incomplete as a tool for non-sales executives wanting to sell something. So the letter was fortuitous.

The problem seems to be that most non-sellers believe that customers or potential customers do want to hear, initially, about their business, how long they've been in business and where the business is going. They often use sales letters to introduce themselves, mainly because they're fearful of picking up the phone. (Read my previous book, *Cold Calling for Chickens*.) But a properly written sales letter can be a great door opener.

Most sales letters are not great. Most amateur sales letters actually "un-sell" their company. The senders are spending postage to send their waste paper to a trash can across town, they might have found it cheaper to throw it in the one at the side of their desk.

Even companies like "Readers Digest" and "Publisher's Clearing House" who *know* how to write sales letters only get a tiny return on them. We're talking 1%–2% maximum and that's just getting the customer to open the envelope. (Actually getting the reader to act on the contents is something else again!) Also, the professional direct-mail organizations send out millions of them and – let's face it – you don't. (Your "mail run" is probably more like 5000 max!) And the person who wrote the letter I have recreated word for word below, clearly needs to read this book. (Only the names have been changed/deleted to protect the innocent!)

Dear Home Owner

"Xxx-Yyy and Staff" is a national estate agency, founded in 1910. We can lay claim to be one of the "famous five" in England. Recently we formed a partnership with the "Zzz" estate agency group in Scotland, so our network of offices now extends to virtually all corners of the United Kingdom. We have been active in Mayfair since 1924 when our first London office opened in 14, Aaa Street (where it remained until it was demolished by a bomb during the Blitz), so our knowledge of your area is unparalleled. Indeed we now cover all the prime markets of central London with eight "Xxx-Yyy" offices and four Ccc and Company offices (our sister company) in the heart of the City's business district.

We are delighted to announce the **opening of a new dedicated W1 sales department at "17 Ddd Street W1 (020 7xx xxxx)** to complement our existing successful letting, commercial and country house departments.

This new department is headed by "James Salesman-Palesman" who has some 25 years experience in the central London marketplace. He would be pleased to advise you on any aspect of buying or selling residential property in the West End, and would be able to provide a free valuation without obligation. In these uncertain "Rocky" times it is more important than ever to know that you are being advised by professionals who have experienced the lows in the market well as the highs. "James" is supported by "Peter Throatwarbler-Mangrove" and "Andrew Smandrew". In addition we have a team headed by "Tom Cleethorpes" FRICS who can advise on all aspects of leasehold enfranchisement.

To celebrate the opening of our Mayfair sales department, we are pleased to confirm that for any instruction received before 30th January 2008, if we are appointed as sole agent for a minimum period of eight weeks, we will reduce our standard commission rate to **1% of the sale price plus VAT.**

We look forward to hearing from you and do not hesitate to pop into our office anytime for a chat and a cup of coffee.

Regards

"James Salesman-Palesman"
"Xxx–Yyy and Staff"

The sound of 4999 of these letters hitting the waste bins of West London at the same time would be deafening. So let us dissect my "one" un-binned letter (out of the 5000) together and have a go at rewriting it. While we do this, we will bear in mind the basic advertising agency rule of thumb when it comes to copywriting: **AIDA.**

Attention

Interest

Desire

Action

(I have marked each point with a key letter)

Dear Home Owner **[A]**

[B] "Xxx-Yyy and Staff" is a national estate agency, founded in 1910. **[C]** We can lay claim to be one of the "famous five" in England. Recently we formed a partnership with the "Zzz" estate agency group in Scotland, so our network of offices now extends to virtually all corners of the United Kingdom. **[D]** We have been active in **[E]** Mayfair since 1924 when our first London office opened in 14, Aaa Street (where it remained until it was demolished by a bomb during the Blitz), so our knowledge of your area is unparalleled. Indeed we now cover all the prime markets of central London with eight "Xxx-Yyy" offices and four Ccc and Company offices (our sister company) in the heart of the City's business district.

[A] If you hope that any prospective customer is going to act on your letter you must use their name at the start. A person's name is their most important possession so, to grab their **A**ttention, you MUST use it at the opening. "Dear Home Owner," like "Dear Sir or Madam," or "Dear Managing Director," or any general opening of any sort, and you are asking for your letter to be "chucked". I am NOT a member of the masses! I do not want to feel that I am part of your MASS mailing!

[B] This is a massively long first paragraph for any reader to tackle. It is only four sentences long but what sentences they are. People aren't stupid but they do tend to be both lazy and busy. (Alas, nobody is waiting by their letterbox for your letter) so any thought that your reader will wade through these 126 opening words is optimistic to say the least.

[C] I (your reader) don't care about you, what you are, or when you were founded. It really doesn't interest me. The only thing I need in the first few words is a feeling that you (the writer) understand something about me (your reader). The most persuasive word on the planet is "You"; it doesn't appear once in this opening paragraph.

[D] This second sentence in the first paragraph is 41 words long. Sentences, like paragraphs, need to be kept short and 9–10 words is plenty; 3–5 short sentences in a paragraph is the goal. Think of each sentence and paragraph like a "Classified Advertisement" in your local newspaper. Every word you use must work like a Roman slave for its survival.

[E] And still it goes on: your history! The Second World War ended over half a century ago and I really don't care about Mayfair in 1924 and "The Blitz". There are at least eight old established Estate Agencies in this part of town and some very good "upstart" agents who have only been around for five years or less. And the whole paragraph is packed with Features. Only one Advantage to be seen (at the end of the third sentence) but it won't be because 99.99% of readers will have already binned it by "Dear Home Owner".

> **[F]** We are delighted to announce the **opening of a new dedicated W1 sales department at "17 Ddd Street W1 (020 7xx xxxx)** to complement our existing successful letting, commercial and country house departments.
>
> **[G]** This new department is headed by "James Salesman-Palesman" who has some 25 years experience in the central London marketplace. He would be pleased to advise you on any aspect of buying or selling residential property in the West End, and would be able to provide a free valuation without obligation. In these uncertain "Rocky" times it is more important than ever to know that you are being advised by professionals who have experienced the lows in the market well as the highs. "James" is supported by "Peter Throatwarbler-Mangrove" and "Andrew Smandrew". In addition we have a team headed by "Tom Cleethorpes" FRICS who can advise on all aspects of leasehold enfranchisement. **[H]**

[F] Well I would have stopped reading by now anyway, but this sentence needs a definite mention. "We are delighted to announce" is a classic in the world of "Amateur" sales letters because the writer doesn't appreciate that rest of the world doesn't care about him and his "successful" business. Nor do they care how "delighted" he and his board of directors are about the opening of their new moneymaking machine in "London, W1". The phrase should be banned, by law, from all company "promo" literature in every business in the world. Customers and prospective customers care about themselves and their problems … that's all.

[G] This is a paragraph of names. People I (the reader) don't know, doing things I don't know about. The signee of the letter also tells me, unwittingly, that this is a mass-mailer, boiler-plate letter by stating that, "*The new department is headed by James Salesman-Palesman*". Surely if it was his personal letter to me, a customer whose business he would really value, he'd say, "*I am heading this new department*". Three sentences in this paragraph also contain 31 words each, which doesn't really matter because I've stopped reading anyway.

[H] Keep your words simple! "*Leasehold enfranchisement.*" What? You are not trying to impress the reader with your knowledge of in-house jargon or long legal expressions. I bought my London "leasehold" apartment without once hearing or using the word "*enfranchisement*". Readers are not stupid but they are lazy. Keep it simple.

[I] To celebrate the opening of our Mayfair sales department, we are pleased to confirm that for any instruction received before 30th January 2008, if we are appointed as sole agent for a minimum period of eight weeks, we will reduce our standard commission rate to **1% of the sale price plus VAT.**

We look forward to hearing from you and do not hesitate to pop into our office anytime for a chat and a cup of coffee.

[I] Well there is hope for this amateur sales-letter writer yet; he did finish with a call to **A**ction under the AIDA principle. It is rather a complex one and has caveats but it does have a time limit (*30th January 2008*) which for most readers is an influential element under the influential "Law of Scarcity". No, the thing that concerns me is another old amateur favourite, "do not hesitate" ("*do not hesitate to call me*" "*do not hesitate to pop in*" "*do not hesitate to pick up the phone.*"). Unfortunately the human brain (according to psychologists) cannot hold a negative thought. If I say to you, right now, "do not think of pink elephants!" What immediately comes to mind? Pink elephants. Right?

In the same way if you tell me *not* to "hesitate" my brain doesn't hear the "not". It only hears the "hesitate". I am now programmed *not* to call you. And in the case of the Estate Agent's letter *not* to "*pop in for a cup of coffee*".

Regards

"*James Salesman-Palesman*"
"*Xxx-Yyy and Staff*"

[J]?

[J] And the most important part of the letter is absent altogether. There is no "P.S." Read any successful, professional, sales letter and you will see on 95% of them, at the foot of the page, there is a "P.S." The reason for this is that the foot of the page is where most people look first, when they open any letter which is obviously sent from a company. The human eye tends to go to the bottom of the sheet. And for this reason alone, it is where professional sales people place their most enticing and important benefit and call to **A**ction … *after* the signature.

So let's have a go at rewriting *Mr. James Salesman-Palesman's* letter for him. Remember we need to build the pressure. First we must gain **A**ttention. Then create **I**nterest. After that generate **D**esire. And then call to **A**ction

[Headed paper]

Mr. Robert Etherington
Flat 6, Aldburgh House
Aldburgh Mews
London
W1U 1BT

25th December 2007

Dear Mr. Etherington

Selling your house or flat is not easy. Finding an estate agent you can trust is harder. It is especially true in these tough times. You need all the help you can get. You need a purchaser at the best price who moves quickly to completion.

That's why we have opened a new office in Mayfair. It is two minutes walk from your address and staffed by an expert sales team. They are acknowledged as the best in West London. On average they take 6 weeks or less to sell most properties. Your property and location would be ideal for many of our buyers.

We will also help you rapidly find your next property anywhere in the UK. Our countrywide network of offices and associates are there for you. They will smooth the process by handling every aspect of your freehold or leasehold purchase.

To check our credentials please call us. We can let you have a list of some of our recent clients to contact. They are all within ¼ mile of your address in Mayfair. Once your sale is complete we would be privileged to have permission to add you to the list of satisfied clients. Call 0800 xxx xxxx for a free information packet and put your property sales worries in retreat.

Yours sincerely

James Salesman-Palesman
Partner

P.S. Limited time offer! Sell your house for just 1% of the sale price by calling us before 30th January 2008. Phone us now for FREE on 0800 xxx xxxx.

That's better ... it may not be perfect but we're getting there. Let me show you what makes it more powerful:

Mr. Robert Etherington
Flat 6, Aldburgh House
Aldburgh Mews
London
W1U 1BT

25th December 2007

Dear Mr. Etherington **[A]**

    [B] Selling your house or flat is not easy. **[C]** Finding an estate agent you can trust is harder. It is especially true in these tough times. You need all the help you can get. You need a purchaser at the best price who moves quickly to completion. **[D]**

[A] It is personal. My name is used and *spelt correctly*! (Note: correct spelling helps stop the letter flying into the bin unopened.)

[B] It opens with a "hand-shake"; a statement everyone can relate to which makes the reader feel that I know how he feels.

[C] There are no "30 word sentences" and most of the time I keep each sentence within, or as close as possible to, the target of 10 words.

[D] The "second best" reason to react to this sales letter *now*, goes in this first paragraph. The most important, "act now", benefit comes later on the page.

[E and F] That's why we have opened a new office in Mayfair. It is two minutes walk from your address and staffed by an expert sales team. They are acknowledged as the best in West London. On average they take 6 weeks or less to sell most properties. Your property and location would be ideal for many of our buyers. **[G]**

[E] Notice that each paragraph is indented; it makes a letter much more interesting for the eye and the brain to read.

[F] Notice also, how short the paragraphs are (3–5 sentences) and how all the lines are widely spaced to open-up the whole letter. This makes it look easy and quick (for lazy/busy people) to read.

[G] The paragraphs are full of Advantages and Benefits. What we are and how long we've been around is of no interest to the busy reader. What we DO to solve common problems NOW is the only Interest they may have.

[H] We will also help you rapidly find your next property anywhere in the UK. Our countrywide network of offices and associates are there for you. They will smooth the process by handling every aspect of your freehold or leasehold purchase.

[I] To check our credentials please call us. We can let you have a list of some of our recent clients to contact. They are all within ¼ mile of your address in Mayfair. Once your sale is complete we would be privileged to have permission to add you to the list of satisfied clients. Call free 0800 xxx xxxx for an information packet and put your property sales worries in retreat. **[J]**

[H] Now we are creating **D**esire. We are not only talking about the things we do locally to help. But we're also showing we can remove all the other house buying headaches.

[I] And not only that, we are offering proof that we are very local and know the current situation. And we're offering further proof, through other happy customers' word-of-mouth, that this is all true!

[J] And if all this were not sufficient we are also offering something for "FREE". The word "free" is the most persuasive four letter word in selling. Use it whenever you can. There is no "hesitation" anywhere in the letter either. Call the reader to **A**ction ... now. Tell the reader what to do and remind them why they must; "*put your sales worries in retreat*".

Yours sincerely

James Salesman-Palesman
Partner

[K] P.S. Limited time offer! **[L]** Sell your house for just **1%** of the sale price by calling us before 30th January 2008. Phone us now for FREE on 0800 xxx xxxx. **[M]**

[K] There's your P.S! In the P.S. goes your main act-now benefit for the whole letter. The P.S. is the first place most eyes will look when they open your letter. You grab their **A**ttention. If you act now we will give you something great! We will sell your property for half the normal fee!

[L] The limited time offer introduces "scarcity" into the equation (sale must end Friday) and scarcity is one the great human persuaders.

And, not only that ... **[M]** the telephone call is "free" too. If you include a free phone number for the response you are *seven times* more likely to get a call.

So, following **AIDA** construct your letter:

A. You gained **A**ttention by placing a "free" offer and your "Number 1" benefit in the obligatory P.S. at the end of the letter.

I. You created **I**nterest in the first paragraph by showing that you understood the situation that typical property owners find themselves in ... you acknowledge how they *feel*. You developed that Interest in paragraphs two and three by showing that you are (very) local. And you set out the Advantages and Benefits (solutions) of your complete service. No lone "Features" to be seen. Features make customers think about "the cost".

D. Then in the fourth paragraph you created **D**esire. You did that by offering proof that you CAN deliver what you promise. And you offer more information for FREE (the world's most persuasive four letter word).

A. Having built Desire for your solution you showed the reader how to get the oxygen for themselves. You told them how to take **A**ction ... NOW.

Make sure the whole letter is un-cramped and personal. That it is all contained on one side of a sheet of paper. That the paragraphs are indented and the whole style is light and simple; no long words ... no long sentences ... no long paragraphs.

That's it ... that's how to design a simple sales letter. There is a lot more I could write about mailing-pieces in general but this is plenty for you right now. Most sales letters are door openers. However good you are at writing them, without a follow-up phone call, your conversion rate will not be much more than about .05% ... that's just the way it is. Mr. James Salesman-Palesman's original letter will get a lot less than that.

You now have everything you need to start selling like a Sales God.

Your colleagues will think you're great and your sales staff will think you're wonderful. Not only that but your customers will buy more from you too. What could be better than that?

Good Selling!!

You seem to know something about selling ... I like that in a Sales-Director!

About the author

Bob Etherington has been developing his reputation for sales success since the 1970s, in a career that has spanned many key global markets.

Having begun his sales career in 1970 with Rank Xerox in London, he was quickly headhunted by Grand Metropolitan Hotels and then became a Money Broker in the City. He joined Reuters, the international news and financial information leader in the early 1980s and became a main Board Director for their Transaction Services in 1990, moving to New York in 1994 to take control of their major accounts strategy for US banks. Reuters' international sales to these banks grew rapidly and, as a result, Bob was appointed to organize professional sales training for the entire company.

In 2000, Bob left Reuters and set about expanding SpokenWord Ltd., a London-based sales training business he had already established with his business partner, Frances Tipper.

Today, he leads sales and negotiation programmes for many international, high profile clients and is in demand as an inspiring and charismatic speaker at business conferences around the world. He has also developed several successful US business interests.

Bob is the author of the extremely successful series of books, *Cold Calling for Chickens*, *Presentation Skills for Quivering Wrecks*, *Negotiating Skills for Virgins* and *Selling Skills for Complete Amateurs*.

People wishing to contact Bob can do so by email: robertetherington@yahoo.co.uk or via SpokenWord's website: www.spokenwordltd.com